Innovation and
Social Process

Pergamon Titles of Related Interest

Related Journals*

*Free specimen copies available upon request.

PERGAMON
POLICY
STUDIES

ON POLICY, PLANNING
AND MODELLING

Innovation and Social Process
A National Experiment in Implementing Social Technology

Louis G. Tornatzky
Esther O. Fergus
Joseph W. Avellar
George W. Fairweather
with Michael Fleischer

Pergamon Press
NEW YORK • OXFORD • TORONTO • SYDNEY • PARIS • FRANKFURT

Pergamon Press Offices:

U.S.A.	Pergamon Press Inc., Maxwell House, Fairview Park, Elmsford, New York 10523, U.S.A.
U.K.	Pergamon Press Ltd., Headington Hill Hall, Oxford OX3 0BW, England
CANADA	Pergamon of Canada, Ltd., Suite 104, 150 Consumers Road, Willowdale, Ontario M2J 1P9, Canada
AUSTRALIA	Pergamon Press (Aust.) Pty. Ltd., P.O. Box 544, Potts Point, NSW 2011, Australia
FRANCE	Pergamon Press SARL, 24 rue des Ecoles, 75240 Paris, Cedex 05, France
FEDERAL REPUBLIC OF GERMANY	Pergamon Press GmbH, Hammerweg 6, Postfach 1305, 6242 Kronberg/Taunus, Federal Republic of Germany

HN
65
I65
1980

Library of Congress Cataloging in Publication Data

Main entry under title:

Innovation and social process.

(Pergamon policy studies on politics, policy and modeling)
  Bibliography: p.
  Includes index.
  1. Social change—Research—United States. 2. Action research—United States. 3. Social interaction—Research. 4. Organizational change—United States—Case studies. 5. Social science research—United States.
I. Tornatzky, Louis G. II. Series.
HN65.I65 1980   303.4   80-36809
ISBN 0-08-026303-8

Printed in the United States of America

Contents

Chapter

Preface

Some years ago Kurt Lewin, the renowned social psychologist, articulated the notion of action research. Translated into operational specifics, the concept meant that social scientists ought perhaps to be studying phenomena in settings, and employing methodologies, that might eventually yield some incremental positive social change. The MSU-NIMH Innovation Diffusion Project described in this book is well within that honored tradition.

This project differed considerably from the modal type of research that comes under the rubric of innovation studies. Much in that field has been written about the necessity to study innovation as a "dynamic process." Unfortunately little in the literature expresses the sentiment that the best way to understand any dynamic process is to intervene in it, and to see what happens. That in fact is what was done in this study - one of the very few attempts to experiment actively in innovation dissemination. In the service of studying change, while doing change, the research team gave over 80 workshops, performed several dozen consultations, traveled approximately 244,000 miles, made over 5,000 long distance phone calls, and sent several thousand letters and bits of correspondence. We also came to feel like the Willy Loman of the social science world.

What did we learn from this massive effort? Without going into the specific findings of the study, we did confirm our principal operating hypothesis: that social innovation is facilitated by social interaction. We also confirmed, however, a greater personal truth: that incremental social innovation is a viable route to larger social change. Unlike many of our colleagues who study innovation in retrospect, from afar, or at a level of data aggregation in which the human elements get lost, we actually participated in change.

At bottom then, although the scientific findings from this research may pale in significance over the years, we know that good has come from our expenditure of public funds. In a sense, this book is dedicated to those few hundred formerly institutionalized mental patients who are now living healthier lives and tasting a bit of human freedom as a result of a process of social innovation.

Acknowledgments

This project could not have been undertaken, or completed, without the help of a number of individuals. The Department of Psychology at Michigan State University was the institutional home for the research, and Jack Wakeley, Chairman of the Department, was of inestimable administrative help throughout the duration of the project. Roger Halley, administrative assistant in Psychology, and Marj Curtis, office supervisor, untangled many bureaucratic hassles over the life of the research.

A number of people contributed their wisdom, and moreover some tangible suggestions, during the design, instrumentation, and analysis phases. Jack Wakeley, Raymond Frankman, and Eugene Jacobson read early drafts of the proposal and the work plan, and made many contributions. Ray Frankman was of special assistance during data analysis, particularly in making sense of several highly complex analyses-of-variance.

Several secretaries were employed by the project. Nora Menard survived the hectic early days of heavy travel and considerable correspondence, and retired to Colorado. JoAnn Ohm and Linda Boldt served during mid-passage and were involved in some of the early draft chapters of this book. Marian deZeeuw was an invaluable triple threat person during the period in which the bulk of the book was written. Not only did she type the manuscript, but her well-honed editorial skills and constructive nagging helped us meet our deadlines. Mary Wood had many of the thankless tasks of tying up loose ends concerning tables and graphs.

Neither this book nor this project could have been completed without the assistance of the National Institute of Mental Health, whose Grant 3R01-MH24230 to Michigan State University supported the research. Howard Davis and Susan Salasin of that agency offered encouragement, interest, and moreover, patience throughout the research. We trust that this commitment will not have been ill spent.

Finally, this book could not have been written if nobody ever adopted and implemented the Lodge innovation. To those brave staff, and braver patients, who were involved in the establishment of this innovation around the country, we owe a special note of thanks.

I
An Introductory Overview

1 Innovation, Change, and the Problems of Implementation

SOCIAL INNOVATION: IMAGE AND REALITY

By nature, Americans are an optimistic people. As such, one of the cultural truisms that most of us share is a belief that orderly social change is both possible and desirable, given sufficient material resources and public will. We are inveterate tinkerers without social institutions and have an abiding faith in the slow, steady march of "progress."

These persistent biases have influenced social policy and social science research relevant to the processes of social and technological innovation in at least two ways. One result has been a relative naivete in our thinking about the longitudinal processes involved in innovation. A second major failing has been what Everett Rogers (1975) has called the "pro-innovation bias."

If one considers the processes of innovation, there has been an excessive reliance in the literature on conceptual models that are too linear and rationalistic, and that unjustifiably assume the inevitability of innovation's occurrence.(1) In this view, rational persons will, of course, rationally choose to adopt innovations and replace outmoded social practices. There has been an obvious tendency to ignore the complex social processes and conflicts that accompany change, and to minimize the obstacles to social innovation as a tool for social renewal. As LaPiere (1965) pointed out several years ago, that particular relationship is much more convoluted that we can optimistically assume:

> Although every significant social change begins
> as an innovation, the appearance of innovators and
> innovations does not directly and automatically result

in changes in the social system. No innovation is
ever more than the cornerstone upon which, given
proper social acceptance, a new element of social life
may be erected. . . Seen thus, it is obvious that a
social element does not immediately and automatically
result from an innovation and that the distinction
between the one and the other is multidimensional.
The innovation is new, the social element established; the innovation is accepted only by its innovator, the social element by the society at large;
the innovation is an idea in the mind of the innovator manifest, perhaps, in some material tool or
device, while the social element is a functioning part
of the social system, incorporated in the culture and
embodied in the personalities, practices, or equipment of the members of the society.

Regarding the "pro-innovation bias," the point to be made is
very simple: we ought not to assume uncritically that the
dissemination, adoption, and implementation of innovations is
inevitably desirable for society. The atrractiveness of innovating per se needs to be separated from its effects. This
issue has particular relevance for social technologies, as
opposed to material technology, and for the research to be
presented in this book. The case is aptly made by Rogers
(1975):

> The classical diffusion model assumed that
> everyone in the audience should adopt, that diffu-
> sion rates should be rapidly increased, and that
> rejection was an undesirable and/or irrational deci-
> sion. This pro-change bias may have been justified
> in the case of many of the agricultural innovations
> that were originally studied, and which strongly
> flavor our conception of the diffusion process.
> After all, hybrid corn was a highly profitable in-
> novation for farmers.
> But many innovations do not have such a uni-
> versal usefulness, and such innovations may be
> appropriate for adoption only by some individuals,
> and by some organizations. Methadone maintenance
> and dial-a-ride and mace are not in the same league
> of relative advantage as hybrid corn.

Given the fragility of social system technologies, and the
ephemeral nature of their positive benefits, concern for identifying the processes of innovation is doubly apt. These two
themes will color this chapter and ensuing sections of this
book. Not only do we need to be concerned with the effects
of social innovations, we also need to examine, with appropri-

ately precise methodologies, the ways in which the link between social innovation and beneficial social change can be strengthened.

The Bumbling Giant: Public Service Programs

One of the premises of a "pro-innovation" stance is that, over time, the institutions of a society will be renewed or replaced by new and effective alternative practices, yet one recurrent feature of any criticism of public bureaucracies is the notion that we are in the midst of uncontrolled growth in the number, kinds, and prices, of government service programs. The image of layer piled upon layer of service programs is not only metaphorically, but also literally appropriate.

For example, one may merely look at gross increases in taxation and government expenditures over the past 40 years, and the last 20 years in particular. The inescapable conclusion is that government has clearly become the growth industry of recent decades. Considering such gross indices as percentage of increase in government expenditures as a portion of the gross national product, number of employees involved, and total dollars expended for government services, the evidence is persuasive. For example, data cited by Kirst (1979) indicate that state and local expenditures as a percentage of personal income have doubled since 1948. Similarly, the number of state and local employees has doubled, as a percentage of population, since that time.

Perhaps more impressive than fiscal data is the simple fact that these significant increases in dollars also represent an underlying growth in the absolute number of programs and bureaucracies. To indulge in personification, government agencies have nearly attained immortality through cloning. In an illuminating recent study, Kaufman (1976) asked the very question, "Are government agencies immortal?" His findings, based on a 50-year retrospective review of the organizational structure of several federal departments, indicated that they are indeed immortal and that much of the growth in federal programs comes from within the bureaucracy rather than because of an explicit legislative mandate.

Since government programs are so resilient, every program, either from this generation or from years past, makes a continuing and growing demand on public expenditures. Of course, growth might be acceptable if there were corresponding evidence to indicate that the multiplication of social programs had resulted in a commensurate increase in the alleviation of social problems, or a significant increase in confidence in public institutions. Unfortunately, as will be discussed below, this has not occurred. Perhaps the current nostalgia for the 1950s is the most visible evidence of a collective disenchantment within the body politic.

Some Specific "Innovation" Failures

Because this book is, among other things, about effecting meaningful innovation and change in mental health institutions, we will touch briefly here on how well these intitutions have dealt with a significantly problematic population of clients left in their charge - the chronically mentally ill.

Three decades ago, our public mental hospitals were virtual warehouses of chronic patients. Since treatment modalities for the acutely mentally ill were also lacking in quality and quantity, the acutely ill, through a process of gradual acculturation to institutional life, came to be enlisted into the armies of the chronic. However, during the 1950s, pharmacological developments in the form of phenothiozine drug treatments made possible many startling and hopeful changes in the behavior of members of this problem group. For the first time, massive discharges of the chronically ill from hospitalization became conceivable; correspondingly, the development of supportive after-care facilities in the community became eminently desirable if not mandatory. This was a circumstance in which the introduction of one technological innovation exacerbated the need for complementary social innovations.

Unfortunately, the problem of the chronically mentally ill is still with us. The programmatic response on the part of mental health professionals was less than complete; the "new" community programs proved largely to be failures. Currently, we have an enduring marginal population of discharged patients residing in substandard community residential facilities, who have become one more sub-problem of the urban dilemma. As the recent Presidential Commission on Mental Health (1978) pointed out, many of the dollars intended for solutions to this problem went for naught:

> In the absence of alternative inexpensive housing. . . single room occupancy hotels, especially in large cities, have become the repositories of the unwanted and unfortunate in our society whether they are drug addicts, or welfare clients, or former mental patients. The placement of those discharged from State Institutions into SRO's exacerbates. . . the issue of providing adequate care for deinstitutionalized persons.

The above should not be considered an isolated example of a public policy shortcoming. In recent years, a chronicle of such failures has been extensively documented in the literature of social program evaluation. (For example, Chalupsky and Coles [1977] report a longitudinal evaluation of the effects of a set of educational "innovations" implemented in the 1960's. The net effect on achievement and related indices, as evidenced in

a national sample of schools and children, was nil.) The
summary conclusion of this literature - that not much in the
way of social programming has had unambiguously positive
impact - also leads to two related questions: (1) are there
ways in which we can create innovations that are truly effective? and (2) if we can identify innovations that do work,
how can we use them to reform public bureaucracies? This
research report can be seen as a partial response to these
questions.

CREATING SOCIAL INNOVATIONS THAT WORK

A Model

Although we have spent some time in a pessimistic review of
past social innovation failures, our intent was not generally to
disabuse the reader of his or her faith in newness per se.
Innovations, or new programs, or "fresh policy initiatives," are
not necessarily equivalent to effectiveness, but they can be,
given an appropriate process of development and nurturance.
We have strenuously made the point that social technologies
and innovations are inherently fragile creations. We would
like to pause for a moment to describe what we see as essential
procedures in that creation. There are systematic methodologies, through which successful innovations can be developed. Since some of the authors have been involved in the
exploitation and advocacy of this methodology for several years
(Fairweather, 1967; Fairweather and Tornatzky, 1977), we shall
describe the nature of that problem-solving process in a
digested form.

Defining the social problem

Before an innovative solution to a social issue can be developed, one must determine the nature of that problem. One
must ask the generic question of what harmful effects that
need to be remedied are occurring for the sub-population with
which we are concerned. For example, what is "not right" for
second-graders with reading problems? How is public welfare
impacting in a negative way on its recipients? And, to return
to the example alluded to above, how are mental health pro-
grammers failing to deliver necessary and effective services to
the chronically ill? In short, given the various stakeholders
in a situation, what set of "problems" receives the greatest
amount of consensus?
    The process of problem identification may occur on a
number of fronts. It may include dispassionate study and
review of current ameliorative programs. It may involve

detached observation of the problem population in vivo. It may demand gathering formal survey data or baseline archival information. It usually calls for an in-depth excursion into the scientific and theoretical literature on the problem. Moreover, in addition to pinpointing the nature of the problem experienced, this process may, it is hoped, lead directly into the next step of what we have termed experimental social innovation. (Coined by Fairweather (1967), the E.S.I. nomenclature is extremely helpful in capsulizing this rational/scientific problem-solving model.)

Creating alternative models

For most social problems, there is typically a standard way to treat a given social malady. For example, treatment of the alcoholic in our society has usually involved some program of abstinence and supportive counseling, either individualistic or group-oriented. In similar manner, the treatment of the elementary school's slow reader usually involves some combination of psychotropic drug and psychotherapy. However, since the use of these "tried and true" institutionalized types of interventions often has a discouraging relationship to desired outcomes, a rational approach might call for a search for alternative models of treatment. One should never make the assumption in social programs that what is currently being done is necessarily the best option.

Alternative models may almost suggest themselves as we learn more about the parameters of the social problem. For example, in an early study of in-hospital treatment programs (Fairweather, 1964), it was found that post-hospital adjustment of the chronic patient seemed to be highly related to employment and a supportive living arrangement. On the basis of these correlational data, it was suggested that a viable alternative model to traditional after-care would be to provide such features within an integrated delivery system. This, in fact, was the alternative model visualized in the creation of the mental health innovation called the Community Lodge (Fairweather, Sanders, Maynard, and Cressler, 1969).

Creating an experimental test

Much of what has been described above could be considered as typically occurring in the development of new social programs. Thus, there is often a period of study, examination of the parameters of the problem, and the conceiving of alternative solutions. However, the next step in a rational-scientific approach to creating innovations differs radically from much of what currently transpires in the policy area. The specific decision aid advocated here is the true experimental comparison of alternative policy models.

Without going into the essentials of experimental method-ology (Campbell and Stanley, 1963; Cox, 1958; Winer, 1971), we will outline some of the essential features of a scientifically respectable experiment. Suppose we have identified two or more alternative models for dealing with a social problem population. We might label these, T (for traditional) and alternatives A_1, A_2 . . . A_n. Such a situation is depicted in Table 1.1 below. [2] By way of example, suppose the social problem is the presence of severe reading deficits for urban elementary school children. The traditional method of dealing with this problem might be an intensive program of remedial instruction on the part of the classroom teacher, or of teacher aides. Some alternatives might be peer tutoring (A_1), home-based parent instruction (A_2), computer-based instruction coupled with monetary rewards (A_3), and so on. In order to obtain a fair comparison between such a set of alternative models, the methodology of choice would be to embark upon a formal experiment.

Table 1.1. Experimental Model for Testing
Social Programs.

Traditional Model	Alternative Model 1	Alternative Model 2	Alternative Model J
Subject T_1	Subject 1_1	Subject 2_1	Subject j_1
Subject T_2	Subject 1_2	Subject 2_2	Subject j_2
. . .	. . .	. . .	. . .
Subject Tn	Subject 1n	Subject 2n	Subject jn

In the situation we have been describing, the subjects would be randomly assigned to the different models. If we could work out an arrangement with a large school district, we might randomly assign third-grade students to one of several alternative programs. At the end of a predetermined time period (e.g., one school year), we would measure relative program effectiveness of the various models in order to make a decision about which one, or which ones, appeared to be significantly different (better and/or worse) from the others.

If, of course, none of the alternatives were significantly better than the traditional model, then rationality would argue for retaining the traditional. It should be obvious that the use of experimentation for the creation of innovations is as often potentially a force for conserving the "tried and true," as it is for creating innovative alternatives. If the ostensible "innovation" is not empirically beneficial, there is no need to replace existing practice.

The decision-making methodology that we have described here is not a mere academic exercise. It has been used, and is increasingly being used, as a way of choosing among social program options. Experimental techniques have been employed in such disparate areas as corrections, mental health, urban planning, and education. In a recent bibliography of such studies (Boruch, 1974), literally dozens of true experimental studies on social policy innovations are listed. (Donald Campbell [Salasin, 1973] has, in the past, expressed a minimal concern for the apparent low level of research utilization shown by bureaucrats and legislators. He cited the paucity of "red-hot findings" as justification for his lack of alarm. The authors feel differently. The stockpile of experimental program evaluations is growing. In addition, although there are still few "red-hot" innovations, we feel that negative findings are equally valuable for use by government decision makers. Too much money has been expended for the "tried and true," which may empirically represent no advantage over doing nothing.) Truly, field application of the methodology is far beyond the developmental stage, and is increasingly becoming a fact of life in various settings. Since this book represents a research on changing mental health institutions, we will describe in some detail the application of that methodology to a recurrent problem in that field.

The Community Lodge: A Prototype Social Innovation

During the 1960s, George Fairweather and his associates initiated a research and development effort focused on the problem of the chronically ill ex-mental patient. This was a social problem area in which the range of alternative program options was quite limited at the time. The traditional type of after-care for the patient discharged from an institution often consisted merely of minimal supportive therapy plus makework activities on a daycare or outpatient basis. Because of an individualistic bias in treatment goals, the patient was encouraged to pursue an "independent living situation," and to participate in the competitive labor market. Needless to say, when operating under such assumptions, the recidivism rate of patients returning to the hospital was rather dismal.

In previous work, Fairweather (1964) had found that post-hospital employment and a supportive living arrangement were both highly important parameters to consider in the post-hospital adjustment of the ex-patient. As a result, in the creation of an alternative program for community care, these aspects were integrated into the system.

The programmatic manifestation of this came to be known as the Community Lodge. The Lodge was a living and working arrangement for the ex-mental patient, in many ways, not unlike a small, communal society. It maximized patient decision-making autonomy, and minimized the directive role of professional staff. The Lodge was designed to be ultimately self-supporting, with each Lodge running and operating its own business from a non-profit corporate base. The prototype Lodge residential facility was established in Palo Alto, California, for a group of approximately 20 male ex-patients from a Veteran's Administration hospital.

Some of the more important operational features of the Community Lodge social innovation are as follows:

1. There is a division of labor, and meaningful tasks, such that each member of the Lodge has a psychological stake in the Lodge;

2. The Lodge must have as much autonomy as possible, with staff involvement being structured to ensure further movement toward autonomy;

3. The norms and activities of the small society must be compatible with those of the larger society within which it is implanted. This means an emphasis on work and productivity;

4. Tolerance for some amount of deviant behavior must be built into the subsystem. In turn, members must learn to discriminate when and where deviance is tolerated;

5. A structured communication feedback mechanism must be devised so that Lodge members can be aware of job performance;

6. Entry and exit from the subsystem must be open, and participation voluntary;

7. Subsystem members should work, and make decisions, as a group whenever possible.

Other, more detailed descriptions of the Lodge innovation are available elsewhere (Avellar, et al., 1978), but the significant extent to which this innovation deviates from normative mental health practice, particularly as applied to the chronic patient, should be obvious to anyone who is familiar with the ethos of the mental health professions.

The prototype Community Lodge was also integrated into a highly sophisticated experimental research design to evaluate its effectiveness over time. Patients were asked to volunteer for the innovative program, and this group of volunteers was then <u>randomly assigned</u> to either the Lodge, or to more traditional types of after-care facilities. These two groups of patients were followed for up to three years subsequent to their assignment to one of the two program options. Data were gathered on community adjustment, employment, and the recidivistic rates of the two groups. Fortunately, this effort at social innovation creations proved to be a resounding success. Figures 1.1 and 1.2 present the data on recidivism and employment for the experimental and control groups respectively in the Lodge experiment.

As can be readily seen from these data, and from our cursory view of the experimental processes, one of the initial questions that we asked above has, we hope, been answered. Yes, it is possible to create social technologies that demonstrably work. It is possible to employ something akin to a rational/scientific decision-making process for choosing among program options. The other question that we raised earlier – how to use these data to influence public bureaucracies – becomes a topic for the rest of this book, and the empirical research to be described here.

In this research the Lodge program will serve as the vehicle for the study of innovation processes. All of the dissemination, implementation, and technical assistance activities to be described in ensuing chapters will be oriented toward advocacy of the Lodge innovation among a sample of public psychiatric hospitals. Before we describe the research, however, we will continue this discussion of some of the more pressing issues in research utilization and innovation implementation.

ON THE UTILIZATION OF SCIENTIFIC KNOWLEDGE

The Community Lodge research described above can be assigned to a very select company. There are probably no more than a few hundred social science research findings that have unambiguous relevance for the world of social policy. The question that needs to be addressed now is how, and why (and also why not) the bridge between potential relevance and actual relevance and action is spanned. How do, or how can the findings of empirical research impact on the practices of public service bureaucracies? This general query raises another series of questions about what we actually mean by "use" and what we are striving for when we use research data to reform public bureaucracies.

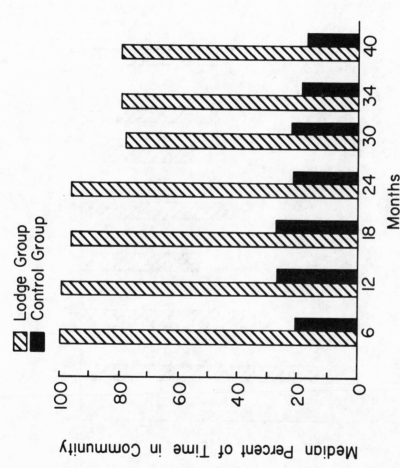

Fig. 1.1. Comparison of lodge and control groups on time in the community

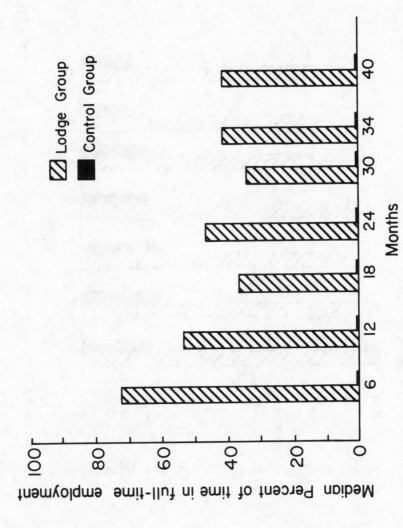

Fig. 1.2. Comparison of lodge and control groups on employment

14

Levels of Utilization

Many observers have concluded that virtually no research ever gets used in a meaningful way by policy makers in the legislative or bureaucratic branches of government (Weiss, 1977), but that general conclusion has been qualified somewhat by recent discussions about what is meant by research utilization.

To return to the Community Lodge example, there are two "messages" or levels of meaning that can be derived, which differ considerably in their degree of abstraction and action relevance, as follows:

1.   A "theme" conclusion might be that supportive community living arrangements, such as the Community Lodge, are in general good things, and by comparison, better than institutionalization;

2.   A more specific, operationalized conclusion to be drawn from the Fairweather Community Lodge research is that a specific program that includes group work, peer decision making, and limited staff role seems to have worked better than a traditional after-care program, and that it ought to be replicated in its entirety in other settings.

Clearly, these two levels of abstraction of the findings have different implications for the definition of "use" of a research finding.   It is obviously easier to use the first general finding than the second, more operationalized one.   The verbal and cognitive incorporation of an abstraction is considerably less demanding than the tangible implementation of its specifics.

Not surprisingly, there is a considerable amount of literature to indicate that indeed bureaucratic and legislative decision makers do make such general use of scientific findings.   For example, Caplan (1977), in a major study of bureaucratic decision makers, found 575 specific instances of knowledge utilization of empirical social science findings. Decision makers are apparently, in a general sense, cognizant of recent themes in scientific research.

Although such findings on utilization may seem superficially encouraging, one can ask what impact such use has had on the actual services being delivered to the clients served by public bureaucracies.   For example, does the incorporation of the general principle of community treatment have clear and tangible implication for the programs being offered to the chronically mentally ill?   The question that needs to be addressed is the degree of linkage between research utilization by "decision-makers" and the actual implementation of an innovation in a delivery setting.   While on the one hand, such utilization may produce increased legislative appropriations for "community" programs of one sort or another, or a shift in a policy position (whatever that means),

the use of findings at that abstract a level is often of very
limited relationship to the quality of direct services offered to
the clientele of public bureaucracies. It is our view that the
link between organizationally and geographically separate
decision makers and operational programs is so tenuous that
utilization of knowledge by such decision makers has no
concrete referent in delivered services.

A clear implication of this conclusion is that the utilization
of scientific knowledge - such as the Community Lodge research - cannot terminate with awareness building among top
level bureaucrats and legislators. At some point, service
providers in the field will have to change what they do on a
day to day basis vis-a-vis their clientele. In short, the direct
and active dissemination of findings, and more important,
operationalized program parameters, to workers in human
service bureaucracies is essential. If, for example, we want
to get mental health workers to provide innovative services to
the chronically mentally ill, we will have to tell them about
innovative programs and explicitly show them how to implement
such programs in their setting. As Williams (1971) has pointed
out in his review of policy research during the days of the
poverty program:

> At the heart of the problem of moving from a
> decision to a program in the field are two complex
> factors: program specification and implementation
> capacity. The first concerns how well specified a
> proposal needing implementation is. Does a decision
> to start a new program in the field rest on a sound
> blueprint for action derived from extensive study
> and testing on a small scale, or from a vaguely de-
> lineated desire to solve a problem? The second
> factor concerns an agency's capability to implement a
> decision once it is made. Does the agency have the
> personnel and organizational capability needed to
> carry out the program as specified in the design?
> When a program does poorly in the field, it is almost
> impossible to disentangle the unique negative con-
> tribution of the design specification underlying the
> decision from the subsequent implementation. But
> together these two problems loom as the biggest
> substantive (as opposed to purely monetary or
> political) hurdles to better social programs.

This research will, in Williams' terms, attempt to alter experimentally the "implementation capacity" of a group of public
service bureaucracies.

Adaptation, Replication, and Program Specification

Even if we assume that an active dissemination strategy is essential for effecting bureaucratic renewal, the question must also be raised as to what is disseminated. Given that one has a prototype that has been validated by experimental research, to what extent should we attempt to obtain exact replications of that model? Should we merely use the model as a springboard for innovation on the part of recipients of the dissemination effort? The issue that we are alluding to here is the question of how much should an innovation be allowed to be adapted by the organization that adopts it. While this has been discussed in considerable detail elsewhere (Glaser and Backer, 1977; Calsyn, Tornatzky and Dittmar, 1977), the gist of that argument should be reviewed here.

The "permissible adaptation" side of the argument rests, to some extent, on the contention that any innovation, no matter how validated it is by research, cannot be spelled out in precise detail. In other words, the essential features of the innovation are not definable in such a way as to be transmitted to new adopters of the program. A corollary feature of the argument is that attempts to reform public bureaucracies ought to proceed on the premise that workers in those organizations need to come to "own" an innovation. They need to have maximum responsibility in deciding its parameters, be active participants throughout the change process, and the like. In short, the dissemination of a "package" innovation is not likely to produce positive results.

The opposite side of the argument, and the one essentially taken by the authors, is that, given adequate research during the development of an innovation, the crucial parameters can be specified, and should be replicated as such. For example, in the case of the Community Lodge program, correlational data over many years had indicated that the crucial features of the Lodge included group-based employment, group decision making, and a limited staff intrusion into the social system. By contrast, replications of the Lodge have varied considerably in many program specifics such as the size and age range of the patient group, in the businesses that have been pursued, and in the specific physical facilities that have been used as a residence. The latter features do not seem crucial, or to deter from the powerful effects of the more core aspects of the program.

That view echoes much of the argument recently elaborated by Boruch and Gomez (1977) in their description of "power theory" as applied to issues of social program evaluation. One of their points is that we need to be able to specify operationally what the "independent variable" (e.g., the social innovation) is, in order to maximize the utility of doing an evaluation in the first place:

Social policy at any level of governance is often
labeled as program and tested as such, when in fact
the operational features of the policy are unknown
and perhaps unknowable. A formal test of the
impact of the policy under this condition is likely to
be an empty exercise.

It follows that if a precise test of a social innovation has taken
place, and positive effects have been found, then the crucial
features of the program need to be maintained in subsequent
replications. The corollary policy issue that is addressed in
the current research is how one can achieve replications of a
demonstrably effective innovation and remain true to the
specific operational features of that innovation. Moreover, can
this be done in a way such that participative planning, and
psychological "ownership" of the innovation is not precluded
by the necessarily directive strategy of dissemination and
technical assistance? Not only must research findings be disseminated and implemented, but those findings ought to be
disseminated about specific programs, in such a way that those
programs are not so modified as to cast doubt on the viability
of the replicates.

The Question of Degree of Program Implementation

In the previous section, we made the argument that specified,
exemplary programs ought to be disseminated and implemented
with fidelity. Not only should this be done to protect the
integrity of the initial prototype, but also because there is
considerable evidence that implementation per se is such an
onerous task that it probably occurs with less frequency than
one might surmise. To elaborate, the distinction needs to be
made here between "verbal implementation" and "behavioral
implementation" of a program. Several investigators have
found that the dissemination of social technology innovations
often produces no more than the former in potential adopters.
A decision to adopt may often result in a mechanical, pro
forma degree of implementation (Gross, et al., 1971; Giacquinta, 1978). Hall and Loucks (1977) have found in educational settings that the adoption of a new program is likely to
be a longitudinal process, and the degree of actual implementation among staff is likely to vary from the negligible to the
complete. It should be intuitively obvious that a program
which is only incompletely implemented can be in no way
assumed to have the same positive effects of the initial
prototype.

Such findings also shed considerable doubt on the thrust
of much of the diffusion of innovation literature of the past.
If one looks at some of the older classical references in the

field (Rogers and Shoemaker, 1971; Havelock, 1971), there is a considerable emphasis on the initial decision-making process, on the communication processes of making people aware of new programs, on persuading potential adopters, and on encouraging individuals to make a decision to adopt an innovation. The innovation process is portrayed as essentially a set of interrelated communicative acts, which result in a yes/no decision to change of not to change.

The thrust of the experiment described in this book is much more complex. We do not see the adoption of social technology as a dichotomous choice point. The initiation of an innovation only begins a tortuous, longitudinal process that may or may not lead to ultimately successful implementation. If, in fact, the course of implementation leads to a distorted "configuration" (Hall and Loucks, 1977) of the original model, we have reason to believe that societal benefits will be attenuated. In a long-term perspective, we also have reason to believe that few model innovations persist to the point of achieving the degree of routinization into everyday bureaucratic practice that might be considered optimal (Yin, 1978). In short, we need to understand the process of implementation that only begins with the initiation of an innovation, and only intermittently results in complete incorporation.

SUMMARY

In a review of the discussion thus far, and its implications for using scientific knowledge to initiate and implement innovations in public bureaucracies, the following points seem particularly pertinent:

1. The overabundance of ineffective, and expensive, human service programs seems to be a pressing issue for public service bureaucracies;
2. It also appears that scientific methodology, particularly field experimentation would yield social program alternatives that would represent a clear increase in effectiveness;
3. In order to effect bureaucratic change via knowledge production, and the creation of alternatives, the utilization of such information needs to be increased dramatically;
4. Utilization cannot be exclusively pursued at an abstract, policymaking level, but needs to be bolstered with implementation at the direct service delivery level;
5. Use at the operational level can only maximize the probability of successful client outcomes, if unadapted replications of a model's prototype are encouraged, and

complete implementation of the model is ensured. The
problem of social innovation is to a significant degree the
problem of implementation, and how to influence the
course of that process.

NOTE

1.   Ron Havelock (1971) has described various such models
of innovation and elaborated many of our criticisms.

2 Social Process and Social Innovation

One of the major unsolved tasks of social innovation that was defined in the previous chapter is to understand how to get organizations to implement reasonable replicates of complex, proven social technologies. In the context of that discussion, we described the development of one prototypical innovation in the area of mental health - the Community Lodge. This book describes a research program designed to effect - and concurrently to study - the implementation of that innovation in a national sample of psychiatric hospitals. However, in order to gain a better appreciation of the yeoman nature of that undertaking, we must first discuss the generic problems associated with implementing program innovations in public bureaucracies, of which the psychiatric hospital is merely one subspecies.

BUREAUCRACIES AND INNOVATION

The Nature of Public Service Bureaucracies

In the previous chapter, we chronicled a fairly ominous population explosion among public bureaucracies. Now we will describe the qualitative nature of these organizations in more detail. In keeping with current social science nomenclature, we have chosen to call such organizations public service bureaucracies. Such organizations are publicly supported, usually bureaucratically structured, and provide an ostensible service to the public at large, or to specific groups of clientele. Under this rubric, such disparate organizations as schools, prisons, hospitals, or methadone maintenance programs, might all be considered public service bureaucracies.

Although there are obvious differences between these organizations, it is worthwhile to consider the commonalities that they share in order to appreciate better the resistance and difficulty experienced in attempts to change such organizations.

All public service bureaucracies tend to mimic many of the features of the ideal legal/rational bureaucracy originally described by Max Weber (1947) nearly 100 years ago. The classical bureaucracy, which public service bureaucracies of course only approximate, is basically structured to maximize rationality and to focus expertise (Litwak, 1961) on the accomplishment of production or service tasks. We will review some of the features of this ideal-type construction.

Some major premises of classic bureaucratic theory are that life is basically rationalizable, that epistemology is basically reductionistic, and that organizational tasks can be a priori deductively subdivided into smaller and smaller subtasks. Correspondingly, one of the most apparent characteristics of the ideal-type bureaucracy is the fact of specialization, and the employment of specialists. In public service bureaucracies, this is translated into convenient fictions, such as the notion that the job description of a psychiatric nurse is radically different from that of a medical technologist, or a physician, or others. However, given specialization in the classical bureaucracy, some coordination of the various specialists is called for. In the ideal-type model, this is supposedly achieved by the use of formal and written rules and established guidelines and procedures. Not surprisingly, many human service bureaucracies do have elaborate procedure and practice manuals for their workers. In order to prevent the idiosyncracies of human personality from intruding on the work setting, a highly formal model of communication is pursued, and a hierarchy of authority is the model of decision-making employed. Since such organizations are so obviously "efficient," the employees reap benefits of security, reasonable material reward, and promotion based on ostensibly objective principles of merit. Merit, of course, is translated into some index of proficiency and knowledge.

Moving from the abstact to the observable, it is clear that public service bureaucracies in the real world differ significantly from the ideal-type bureaucracy that we have just described. Usually the goals pursued by public service bureaucracies are in fact relatively obscure, and the specific tasks performed are not nearly as rationalizable as in the ideal-type construction. As March and Simon (1958) have pointed out, all complex organizations - whether public or private - tend to have multiple sets of goals that are being acted upon at a given point in time. Instead of pursuing a single, well-defined goal, there is more likely to be a blurred mosaic of many goals. Correspondingly, organizations are generally performing an unceasing internal juggling act, in which innovation is only one of many priorities.

There are other radical differences between the ideal-type Weberian construction and the reality of the public service bureaucracy. For example, and implicit assumption of the classical model is that there are clear incentives for efficient operation and productivity. In fact, as has been pointed out (Pincus, 1974), the incentives impinging upon most public service bureaucracies - whether of a financial or symbolic nature - are often those that reward inefficiency or at the very least, the perpetuation of the status quo. For example, if a rehabilitative program successfully rehabilitates all of its clients and conducts a perfect preventive program, it will ultimately go out of business:

> Cases have been reported of a chapter of AA (Alcoholics Anonymous) running out of alcoholics to work on; whereupon the members resumed drinking as there was no other way to continue the game in the absence of people to rescue.(Berne, 1964)

The career profiles of bureaucrats (Downs, 1967) are much more likely to be oriented toward resource aggrandizement than toward "effectiveness," in the usual sense of that term.

All of these deviations of the actual from the theoretical perhaps account for why public bureaucracies, as a species of social organizations, are not nearly as effective in real life as they are in theoretical descriptions. However, even if public service bureaucracies do not replicate the exact substance of the rigorous theoretical model, they do try to emulate the appearance of the classical bureaucratic model. All public service bureaucracies, perhaps ultimately to little avail, try to make their task environment as predictable, and devoid of irrationality, as possible. They do employ specialization (albeit inappropriately at times); they do employ rigid rules and formalistic modes of communication. Employees of schools, hospitals, and prisons are given written job descriptions; they are obliged to use a "chain of command," and so on.

The picture that we have attempted to draw is that of the public bureaucracy trying to maintain a faltering hold on rationality and predictability, in a world that is often irrational and unpredictable. The relationship between this state of affairs, and problems of innovation and implementation, can be made more explicit by considering what innovation is, as an organizational task. A major premise of the research described here is that the task of implementing social innovation is an inherently uncertainty-arousing event for an organization, or more specifically, for its members. As such, it demands a fluidity and flexibility of social processes to cope with that uncertainty. The implication of all this is that the typical public service bureaucracy that we have described is incompatible in structure and function with the processes involved in implementing organizational change and innovation.   The result is a paradoxical situation in which the bureaucracy, by trying to be internally "rational" and predictable, will reject the imposition of externally imposed rationality, such as in the form of social science research and technology.   To understand this paradox better, we need a more complete picture of what change does to public service bureaucracies.

Innovation and Longitudinal Uncertainty

Metaphorically speaking, the implementation of programmatic innovation in public service bureaucracies causes such organizations to experience a great deal of internal upset.   The implementation of innovations within an organization produces uncertainty, and if the innovation is a difficult one to implement, the amount of uncertainty produced will be correspondingly increased.

In spite of classical bureaucratic theory, staff in public service bureaucracies do become quite attached to, and identified with, the operational goals and values of their organization (Merton, 1957).   In short, the job becomes part of them as people.   When a new programmatic innovation is implemented in an organization, traditional values and familiar practices are challenged, and people feel a certain amount of personal discomfort.   To return to the mental health example that will be dealt with in greater detail for the remainder of this book, the Community Lodge explicitly challenged many cherished professional values and norms of psychiatric hospital staff, and the organizational structures and forms designed to reinforce those values.   Most mental health professionals have a deep, abiding belief in the efficacy of "talking therapies," and in the value of intrapsychic insight and other therapies.   In contrast, in the Community Lodge there was a considerably greater emphasis on the social system as the vehicle of treatment, a situation likely to produce resistances among staff who see the underpinnings of their status threatened.

Closely related to organizational values is the set of social and professional roles that people play out in the context of their jobs in public service bureaucracies.   In the implementation of a social innovation, these are likely to be radically disturbed and altered.   In the implementation of the Fairweather Community Lodge, staff were asked to leave the comfort of their carpeted offices and to venture into the community, wrangle with real estate persons, supervise Lodge members' work in a janitorial business, and so on.   (To highlight the problem of challenges to staff roles, we might briefly describe the employment of the "truck test" in this research and in the previous Fairweather, Sanders, and Tornatzky [1974] study. When consulting with a group of hospital staff in the implementation of the Lodge innovation, at some point it became necessary for a staff person to actually get in a pick-up truck or van and start hauling patients from one job to another. This behavioral test rapidly separated the verbal supporters from the more committed advocates.)

In fact, there is a considerable and comprehensive litera-ture on the aspects of innovation that are likely to arouse resistances from the targets of dissemination efforts (Johns, 1973; Rogers and Shoemaker, 1971; Zaltman and Duncan, 1977). These variables include such things as the innovation's com-plexity, relative advantage, and congruity with traditional values. The point of all this is not to become discouraged about the disruptive nature of innovation, but to recognize it as a fact of life. The implementation of innovations stirs things up in public service bureaucracies and arouses what we have loosely described as uncertainty among the staff of such bureaucracies. The implementation of innovations is likely to arouse this feeling in any or all of us; change is difficult.

SOCIAL PROCESS AND SOCIAL CHANGE THEORY:
A LITERATURE REVIEW

A generic hypothesis of this research is that the inevitable aspects involved in the implementation of innovation, which we have labelled uncertainty, can be overcome, or at least coped with, by the facilitation of certain supportive social processes. In order to understand better the rationale for this view, we will pursue several parallel threads of social science literature that we believe lead to similar conclusions.

Organizational Contingency Theory

As was implied in our previous discussion of classical bureau-cratic concepts, Max Weber is not the last word in describing how organizations do or should work. Anyone who has progressed beyond an introductory social science course has probably run across that old chestnut called the Hawthorne Study (Roethlisberger and Dickson, 1947). As will be re-called, the principal finding of that study was the "Hawthorne effect," in which a group of workers, ostensibly under scrutiny for ways to increase their assembly line productivity, tended to respond in rather aberrant ways to the stimuli applied to them. In short, regardless of whether lighting was increased or decreased, or breaks were increased or de-creased, productivity tended to increase over the duration of the study. At the very least, this study largely destroyed the credibility of the traditional bureaucratic model of organizational functioning, in which personnel were held to be specialized automatons in pursuit of material gain and security.

Since that early study, and as a result of other classic studies during the interim (Bowers and Seashore, 1971; Lawrence and Lorsch, 1967), a more sophisticated counter-revolution in organizational theory has emerged in the last 10 to 15 years. Following current usage, we will label this group of theorists as representatives of "organizational contingency theory," and describe some of the main features of this point of view.

Basically, organizational contingency theory asserts that complex organizations, or in our case public service bureaucracies, are typically confronted with more than one kind of task. Task here is construed in a very loose sense to incorporate such aspects as the total task environment, the specific technology employed, the social environment of the work setting, the clientele served, and the like. At any rate, some tasks may be considered uniform (Litwak, 1961), and other tasks can be considered basically non-uniform. The former group of tasks comprises those things that are repetitive, rationalizable, appropriate for task specialization, or in short, highly congruent with the assumptions underlying the classical bureaucratic model. The other tasks are those which are non-uniform, idiosyncratic, nonrepetitive, involve questions of value, or are, to return to the argument we are describing, ones that are inclined to arouse uncertainty among organizational personnel. These are tasks that are better handled in a nonbureaucratic, informal setting. The specific nomenclature adopted by the various organizational contingency theorists varies one from the other (Galbraith, 1973; Thompson, 1967; Perrow, 1972; Lawrence and Lorsch, 1967), but the message is essentially the same: depending upon the task confronting an organization, the structure and processes employed in the accomplishment of that task should differ in order to maximize effectiveness.

This general theoretical view seems to have relatively explicit implications for our problem of implementing organizational innovations. The task of change can be considered as an excellent example of a non-uniform task confronting an organization. The process of innovating is not covered in job descriptions, nor is it covered by written rules and standardized procedures. As such, the type of organizational structure and processes employed by an organization to cope with change need to be compatible with the task demands of that situation. On the bureaucratic/nonbureaucratic continuum, it would seem that the task of innovating would call for a nonbureaucratic solution. An organization - or subunit thereof - which is more informal, interactive, less hierarchical, and not bound by rules, procedures, and professional roles, would be able to cope with innovation more effectively.

Comparative Organizational Studies

There is a considerable literature, either of a case study or correlational nature, designed to describe organizational variables related to proclivity to change. Without going into great depth in this literature, we will review some of the more familiar studies.

The classical study in this genre is Burns and Stalker (1961). While not specifically a study of public service bureaucracies, it has direct relevance for our problem. These investigators began with a relatively small sample of British corporations, operating in the private sector. An attempt was made to classify the corporations according to how innovative they were, which was considered to mean the degree to which they used new technology, new manufacturing techniques, and other deviations from the status quo. In addition, the researchers attempted to do fairly in-depth studies on the structure and functioning of each of the organizations in the sample. This involved direct observation, some interviewing, and a generally systematic observational data-gathering strategy. The upshot of the study was that they came to classify the organizations as "organic" or "mechanistic" in form and function. The latter would be much more bureaucratic in terms of the classical Weberian typology, while the former would be much more informal, less hierarchical, and "looser," organizationally speaking. Burns and Stalker found that the organic form of organization seemed to be clearly related to a greater utilization of innovation and advanced technology.

In another study attempting to relate organizational variables to change, Hage and Aiken (1970) studied a sample of social service agencies. Their dependent variable was the amount of new programs engaged in by the agencies in the sample. Their findings were quite reminiscent, albeit couched in a different and more restricted terminology, of those in the previous study. Briefly, the implementation of organizational innovations seems to be related to a less hierarchical and less "bureaucratic" organizational structure and form. Other findings in this tradition seem similar (Havelock and Havelock, 1973). The general finding is that at a very gross level, innovation and change seem related to organizational processes that deviate from the classical bureaucratic model, in the direction of being more open, less hierarchical, more organic, and the like.

Experiments in Group Decision Making and Participation

There is considerable literature in this area, both of a laboratory and field-experimental nature. Perhaps the most classic is the Lewin (1958) study of group decision making on the part of housewives during World War II. This relatively crude, naturalistic experiment was at the same time a study in the social influence process, and an attempt at social influence. Specifically, because of meat shortages brought on by national defense needs, housewives needed to make greater use of the less desirable cuts of meat. This led quite conveniently to an experiment testing various techniques of social influence, with a sample of housewives. The principal finding of the study was that if housewives had an opportunity to discuss the program, and to make a public commitment in front of their peers to purchase glandular meats, then they were more likely to exhibit real attitudinal and behavioral change. Although there were several methodological flaws in the study, and some of the findings have been qualified by subsequent research (Bennett, 1955), it is of interest to the problem at hand. Perhaps more directly relevant is another classic and influential field experiment by Coch and French (1948). This study, conducted in an industrial setting, was an attempt to determine the most efficacious way of getting production line workers to accept new changes in manufacturing techniques. To return to the nomenclature of this book, an attempt was being made to implement an organizational innovation. The conditions involved in the experiment included passively informing workers of the intended changes, and more actively involving them in participative discussions of one sort or another. The general finding of the study was relatively clear cut. The effect of participative discussion was to enhance the likelihood that the innovation would be accepted without marked resistance.

Once again, although the specific findings of the study have been qualified and sometimes only partially replicated (French, et al., 1960), the general findings are still important. Participative discussion and decisionmaking seem somehow to be related to acceptance of new practices.

Social Comparison Theory and Research

Although emanating from a fairly narrow and academic tradition, and not directly related to an organizational context, some of the concepts and findings of social comparison theory may be relevant to our discussion. In Festinger's (1954) initial description of social comparison theory, it was held that one of the prime functions of social interaction was to enable people to use other people to define their social environment. A corollary to this general position would be that in situations in which uncertainty about one's social environment is enhanced, there would be an even greater need to obtain feedback and clarity from other individuals.

A fascinating series of studies reported by Schachter (1959) tends to support these notions. In effect, it appears that the affiliation motives of people are to some degree enhanced by the need for uncertainty reduction in social situations of stimulus ambiguity. For example, if subjects of a laboratory experiment are informed that they will shortly be given an electical shock, and are then given the option to wait either alone or with another person, they generally will choose the latter alternative. Research subsequent to this group of studies has elaborated upon this general finding, but the basic concept of social comparison has relevance for the problem of implementing organizational innovations. To the extent that organizational innovations enhance people's need for uncertainty reductions, social processes that emphasize <u>interpersonal contact and interaction</u> will enable people to cope more effectively with that situation.

The Rhyme and Reason of Organizational Development

In the previous reference to the Hawthorne studies, it was pointed out that this study was one that indirectly led to the development of organizational contingency theory. Organizational development theory and practice are more direct descendant of the Hawthorne findings. Organizational development has taken the simple fact that informal groups, human communication, interpersonal trust, and friendships are all important aspects of organizational functioning, and has developed this fact into a view of what organizations <u>should</u> be.

The thrust of organizational development theory and practice is to create organizations that are ostensibly better at problem solving and are more humane, more open, and more participative. In turn, this has led to the development of intervention practices (Morris and Sashkin, 1976) designed to provide organizations with intensive consultation on improving their planning, decision making, and communication. Some of the specific tactics used by OD include such disparate activities as encounter groups, in which members of an organization may go to an offsite location and let down their hair, expose their psyches, and gain more interpersonal openness and communication, and survey feedback, in which a formal survey is taken of organizational members, and data is fed back to said members in the hoped of enhancing collective insight into organizational problems. In actuality, the list of specific tactics is nearly endless (Pfeiffer and Jones, 1969;

1970a; 1970b; 1973), but there are some common threads running through all organizational development interventions. French and Bell (1973) list the following points of similarity:

1. Organizational development is designed to be a re-educative strategy, that educates staff members to become more open, communicative, and interactive;
2. It is a technique which focuses on the naturally occurring groups and cliques in organizations;
3. It is a set of techniques that emphasizes confrontation, insight, and "psychological" routes to change;
4. It emphasizes group decision making, and group planning of organizational activities;
5. It emphasizes enhancing the problem-solving capacity of the organization.

We could perhaps extend this list, but this gives the general gist of the OD approach. However, beneath the variety of specific techniques, and the occasionally over-blown rhetoric, there are some themes that are of direct relevance to our problem of implementing programmatic innovations in human service bureaucracies. There is an explicit recognition that classical, rigid, bureaucratic forms are inappropriate for a responsive organization. There is an explicit emphasis on creating the "changeable" organization as an end in itself. Clearly these are all points of view that are relevant to helping bureaucracies cope with the problems of change.

An Empirical Precursor

Before ending this discussion, and stating the hypotheses of the current study, we must describe a more direct lineal antecedent of this research. During the period 1967-71, another dissemination experiment was fielded by members of the current research group (Fairweather, Sanders, and Tornatzky, 1974). The sample for that study was a group of 255 state and federal psychiatric hospitals across the United States. Lasting four years, the project went through the various steps of approaching the target hospitals, attempting to persuade them to adopt the Community Lodge innovation, and providing consultation assistance during implementation. A two-phase research design was employed.

Phase I was a 3x5x2x2 factorial experiment, designed to investigate various persuasion media modalities, ranging from a mailed-out brochure to an interpersonnally intensive dem-onstration program. This was crossed with an examination of entering the organizations at various levels of their hier-archies, and certain demographic blocking variables. Aside from the experimental results of Phase I of the study, a series of correlational findings have particular relevance for this study. There was a strong and recurrent relationship between participative decision making and the degree of change observed in the sample of hospitals. In effect, the extent to which participation was bred into the organization through the inclusion of more lower status staff, more online ward staff, and the like, the greater was the likelihood that change would be observed in the form of movement toward adoption of the Community Lodge.

During Phase II of the previous dissemination study, a related sample of 25 volunteer hospitals was given various types of technical assistance/consultation assistance. A two-cell experimental design compared the provision of onsite consultation versus the use of a do-it-yourself written manual. Although the finding that person to person consultation was significantly superior to the manual condition is of importance in itself, some other fragmentary observational/correlational data are equally relevant for the current study. One particularly interesting finding was the fact that those hospitals which moved further toward actual program implementation were those in which the adopting group of staff functioned as a more coherent group in terms of their interaction patterns and degree of group affect. In short, there was more of a coherent group structure, more open group communication, and a greater sense of group destiny.

The common themes, as we see them, of the previous pages of discussion are summarized below.

THE CURRENT STUDY

Three Generic Hypotheses and One Logistical Imbroglio

On the basis of the above literature, three related hypotheses in the current research were advanced as follows:

1. To the extent that broad-based participative decision making can be encouraged in target organizations, there will be a greater likelihood of movement towards implementation of the organizational innovation;
2. Given that the implementation process is in many ways incompatible with rigid bureaucratic structures and modes of interaction, attempts substantially to change the nature of the adopting group or organization into a more interactive, less bureaucratic form are likely to enhance implementation of social innovation;
3. Given the uncertainty-arousing nature of organizational innovation, consultation and technical assistance designed to reduce, or cope with, felt uncertainty will produce a greater degree of implementation of social innovations.

Despite the obvious inherent wisdom of the above hypotheses, their implications for action strategies, which could be tested in field experiments, are somewhat obscure.

The reason for this is quite simple: most public service bureaucracies do not want to undergo change. They are not likely to "sit still" while one attempts to tinker with their decision-making processes, or the nature of subgroups within their organization. Also, since the experiments described in this book deal with a national sample of public psychiatric hospitals, we should point out that these organizations are not exactly wellsprings of innovation and change.

This creates logistical difficulties for viable experiments in change. Since the organizations in this sample were also by definition resistors to change (see p. 38), the degree of contact that could be possible with such organizations would be fleeting. How then to manipulate interventions, and consultations, in ways that one could remotely expect to impact on organizational processes such as participation, communication, group problem solving, and the organization's ability to cope with the uncertainties of innovation?

An Overview of the Book

The remainder of the volume is devoted to describing researches aimed at unravelling the issues discussed in this and the previous chapter.

Chapters 3, 4, and 5 describe a national experiment comparing various technical assistance tactics designed to impact on organizational processes and decision making, and ultimately on the implementation of an innovation. Chapter 3 is devoted to a description of the methods and procedures of that experiment. Chapters 4 and 5 present results from the dissemination and implementation phases of the project.

The remaining chapters deviate significantly from the typical innovation study of an identified "change agent," facilitating dissemenation and implementation activites. From the study described in chapters 3-5, and from the previous Fairweather, Sanders, and Tornatzky (1974) research, we became concerned about a related policy issue, that is, what is the extent to which service providers themselves are, or can become, involved in innovation processes? These chapters describe a set of observational and experimental studies addressing the issue of indigenously-initiated innovation, and various attempts to facilitate that process.

The last chapter will present a summary of results, and a set of policy recommendations derived from these data.

II

A National Experiment in the Implementation of Innovation

3 Designing an Experiment in Organizational Innovation

Reflecting the issues articulated in the previous two chapters, the goal of the present experiment was to find ways to manipulate organizational processes and, to some extent, structures, as a means of facilitating the implementation of a social innovation, the Community Lodge. This led to a two-phase research design: Phase I attempted to enhance participative decision making during the initiation state of implementation; Phase II involved the use of organizational development techniques as an adjunct to an ongoing, longitudinal process of technical assistance.

As discussed earlier, it is patently insufficient merely to make top level administrators of bureaucracies aware of effective social innovations. Since it is the sine qua non of administrators to make their organizations as predictable as possible through the use of specialization, rules, formal lines of communication, and the like, interest in innovation per se is understandably limited. An administrator of a bureaucratic organization may be made aware of an effective social program, but the probabilities are low that he or she will spontaneously respond by incorporating it into organizational practice; to do so is to introduce considerable ambiguity and uncertainty into such a system. How, then, does one initiate innovation processes in a structured public service bureaucracy, given the type of unilateral, or quite restricted, decision making usually present? Our attempts to produce, or enhance, participative decision making during Phase I are a preliminary exploration of this problem.

Other research that we have reviewed on implementation suggests that implementation is a tenuous and tortuous process that may impose considerable longitudinal stresses on the organizational vigor of the adoption group. Facilitation of the communication process only during the initiation stages is in-

35

sufficient to insure innovation implementation. The literature argues for the necessity of creating more substantial changes in organizational processes and structures that will support the implementation of the innovation in the bureaucratic setting. The coupling of organizational development techniques with a more content-oriented technical assistance effort is the purpose of the Phase II research.

Parenthetically, there is relatively little empirical, particularly experimental, research on effective ways to introduce innovation into a bureaucratic organization. This is doubly so when the intervention is of necessity brief and initiated by actors external to the organization. Thus, to a significant degree, much of this research breaks new ground. This chapter will describe the research design and methods used to encourage a national sample of state and federal (Veteran Administration) psychiatric hospitals to implement the Community Lodge progam, a noteworthy example of social technology. The study consisted of two separate experiments, both designed to impact on organizational process and structure. The underlying assumption of both of these studies is that an outside consultant can influence such changes within an organization, and through this intervening process, overcome the normal and expected resistances to innovation, and move the organization toward implementation.

GETTING PAST THE GATEKEEPERS:
THE PHASE I EXPERIMENT

Phase I of the research involved dissemination activities that began with our initial contact with the sample of hospitals, continued through workshop training, and ended with a decision by the organizations whether or not actually to implement the Community Lodge program.

The experimental plan employed was a 3x2x2 factorial design, which is depicted in figure 3.1. All of the factors were intended to impact on participative decision making during this initiation phase of the intervention. The three factors and the associated hypotheses are as follows:

1. Breadth of Involvement in Decision Making: this was an attempt to manipulate the number of people (Few versus Many) involved in early decision making relative to the innovation.
   Hypothesis 1 - The more people involved in early initiation decisions, the more likely decisions for innovation will result.
2. Intensity of Involvement in Decision Making: this was an attempt to manipulate the quality and intensity of group

discussion and interaction relative to the innovation. It involved High and Low Group Enhancement conditions.

Hypothesis 2 - The more discussion and interaction relative to the innovation, the more likely decisions for innovation will result.

3. Organizational Role of Decision Makers: this factor represented an attempt to manipulate the organizational roles and statuses of those involved in decision making relative to the innovation (Staff/Administrators/Staff and Administrators). This structural decision-making manipulation was an attempt to deviate from administratively-controlled, unilateral decision making that seems to discourage innovation.

Hypothesis 3 - Greater involvement of non-administrators would more likely yield decisions for innovation.

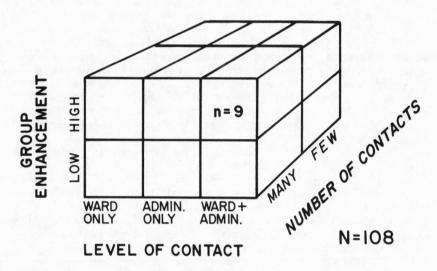

Fig. 3.1. Phase I design: approaching and persuading

Subjects

Hospitals

A sample of 108 psychiatric hospitals was selected for the study from a national population of 255 institutions. (In fact, this was not the entire national population of Veterans Administration and state psychiatric hospitals. As described in the earlier study [Fairweather, et al., 1974], a handful of

hospitals had been eliminated for various sampling and design
considerations. However, this group of 255 represented nearly
90 percent of the national population at the time of this
study.) As a result of an earlier 1967-1971 dissemination
research (Fairweather, Sanders, and Tornatzky, 1974), all of
these 255 hospitals had been assigned a "changeability" score
of one, two, or three (low change to high change respectively)
on the basis of the degree-of-implementation achieved in
response to the experimental interventions in that prior study.
Using these results, the researchers excluded all hospitals
with a change score of three, which elminated 25 hospitals that
had had a considerable amount of contact with the previous
research team. It should be noted that this "changeability"
score was not a dependent variable for the current study, but
a matching variable, based on prior data, for selection at the
sample. Also eliminated were any other hospitals which had
had a consultation or training contact with a member of the
current, or prior, research team, and hospitals which were
located in the state of Michigan, the site of the project. This
yielded a "population" of 168 hospitals from which the sample
was drawn. (At the time that this sample was drawn, members
of the research team were involved in discussion with Michigan
state officials in consideration of a possible statewide training,
dissemination, and consultation project. For obvious reasons
of sample biasing, Michigan institutions were thus excluded at
this time from the sample. As a result, several Michigan
hospitals were involved in the site visit experiment described
in chapter 9.)

Hospitals were then matched into homogeneous groups on
the basis of the previously described change score, and in
terms of the intensity of prior contact (mailed brochures,
workshops, or demonstration projects) they had received in
the previous study. Hospitals within each group were then
randomly assigned to one of the 12 experimental cells. The
total N was 108 (n = 9 per cell). The geographic diversity of
the sample is shown in figure 3.2.

In retrospect, this elaborate matching and elimination
procedure based on prior contact was probably unnecessary.
At least five years had elapsed since any previous contact with
the vast majority of the hospitals, and turnover and memory
loss presented the researchers with a virtual tabula rasa.

Individual respondents

The number of individual staff respondents to measurement
instruments ranged from an N of 318 for the questionnaire
distributed to initial contacts, to an N of 1620 staff for the
later measures.

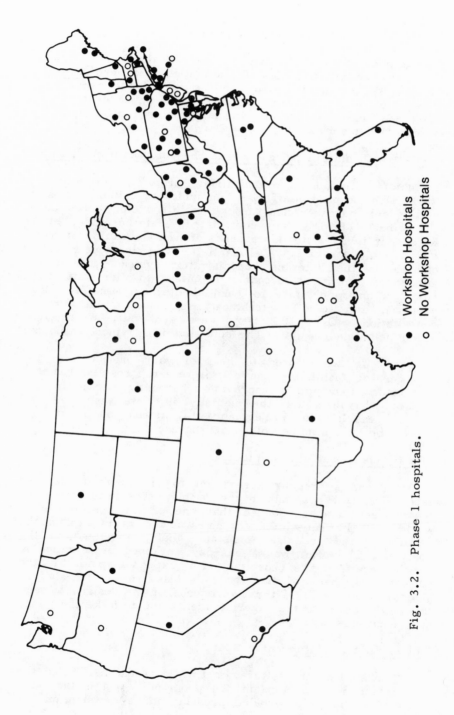

Fig. 3.2. Phase 1 hospitals.

• Workshop Hospitals
○ No Workshop Hospitals

39

General Procedures

In describing the procedures performed during the Phase I research, we will first describe activities that were common to all hospitals, without regard to the cell of the experimental design to which they were assigned. The subsequent sections will then describe the idiosyncratic features of each of the manipulated factors.

Contact with state departments and the veterans administration

In abiding by normal organizational protocol, our intent to work with hospital staff was communicated initially to state and federal bureaucracies through an introductory letter about the project. Prior to any contact with state hospitals, letters were sent to all state departments of mental health that had a hospital in the sample. A similar letter was also sent to senior officials in the Veterans Administration system. The letters announced our intent to contact hospitals, to offer staff at the hospitals an opportunity to learn about the Community Lodge program, and to offer technical assistance in the form of consultation. Over 30 letters were sent out; we received seven acknowledgments. The following is a typical response:

> We are pleased to hear of your project con-
> cerning facilitating the use of research results that
> could be helpful in improving treatment programs in
> our hospitals for the mentally ill. We wish you
> success in your project and will, indeed, be happy
> to be kept informed of your progress.

Initially contacting the hospitals

A letter and a brochure were sent to the superintendent of each of the 108 hospitals in the sample. The letter explained the project, and announced that one of the research staff would call the superintendent in a few days to explain the details of the technical assistance being extended to the hospital. The offer was a one-day workshop presentation at the superintendent's hospital with expenses paid by the project. Members of the research team were randomly as-signed, within each of the twelve cells of the design, to send this initial letter to the superintendents and to make the phone call describec below.

Call to the superintendent

Two weeks after the letter was sent, a researcher called the superintendent to re-explain the program. At this time, the researchers carefully avoided pressing for a decision on the offer of the workshop.

Two of the experimental manipulations were initiated during this phone call. The researcher asked the superintendent for the <u>names</u> of other staff to send information to, and with whom to <u>discuss</u> the program. Depending on the condition, the request was for either <u>Few</u> or <u>Many</u> names, and for personnel who were either line <u>Staff,</u> <u>Administrators,</u> or a group that was a combination of both (see pp. <u>44</u> to <u>46</u> for a more detailed elaboration of the manipulations). The researchers gave the following explanation for these requests:

It has been our experience in working with hospitals that, in addition to the superintendent, other members of the professional staff like to be involved in some initial information sharing. We hope you will agree that consideration of such a program requires interested staff involvement. Therefore we would like to contact, and send the brochure that you recently received, to several other staff members in your hospital in order to provide them with information and answer any questions they may have about the program. In other words, we would like you to defer the decision about the workshop until after we've shared the information with the other staff.

These manipulations proved to be workable. Only 14 of the 108 superintendents refused to release staff names. Eleven of the superintendents flatly refused to discuss the matter with the caller, let alone release any names. One superintendent said he had the best program in the country, and his staff wouldn't be interested in any new programs unless he <u>told</u> them to be interested. When asked if he would please complete a brief questionnaire, the superintendent said he would do it if the researcher would pay him $1000 per hour. Needless to say, this was beyond the resource constraints of the research project. The three remaining superintendents who refused to release any staff names did read the materials and presumably did discuss the entry request. One such hospital sent the following answer:

In response to your recent letter regarding a hospital-community treatment program for mental patients, please be advised that this Institute has its own research and training programs exclusively. We are, therefore, unable to participate at this time in your collaborative program.

Contact with other staff

After the superintendent released the requested names, the researchers called the identified staff members, explained the program to them, offered to send a brochure (which they all accepted), and informed them that the institution would be contacted in two weeks for a decision about the offer to present a workshop. All staff received a letter and a brochure as a follow-up to the researchers' telephone conversation with the superintendent. The superintendents received a letter informing them that the researchers had contacted their staff, and a carbon copy of the letter to their staff was enclosed.

Workshop decision

At the end of two weeks, the researchers wrote to the hospitals and asked for a decision about the workshop offer. They reiterated that there would be no cost to the hospital, that all of the consultant's expenses would be paid by the research project, and that the hospital was under no obligation to adopt the program. If no reply was received within two weeks, the researchers telephoned for a decision.

Eighty out of 108 hospitals agreed to receive the one-day workshop. Some hospitals that turned down the workshop offer explained that staff were interested, but that timing was not right for the hospital. Two not infrequent explanations were that the hospital was preparing for the site visit from the Joint Commission on the Accreditation of Hospitals, or that the administration was undergoing some "reorganization". An unexpectedly candid reason was given by a remote rural hospital in the west:

> First, some feared your workshop might inflate staff expectancies unrealistically. This inflation of hopes and the subsequent letdown are demoralizing . . . A certain trepidation was expressed about meeting with a high-powered group of psychologists. These fears probably arise from our extreme isolation in rural Hicksville. Regrettably, we're out of the mainstream of academic thought, and some feared that intervention from outside might expose our ignorance.

If the decision was yes, the researchers again randomly assigned one of the three research team members to act as the consultant and make the workshop presentation. The consultant called the hospital and set up a workshop date, asked for necessary audio-visual equipment, and also asked the hospital to send a list of workshop participants at least two

weeks prior to the workshop date. This request was to
ensure that some planning took place prior to the workshop,
and also led to an instrumental part of another of the experimental manipulations (see pages 46 to 50). The contact
rarely failed to give the researchers a list of participants
before the mailing deadline. If the list was not received by
the deadline, the consultant telephoned the hospital contact for
the list of participants' names. A packet was mailed to all the
people on the list.

A confirmation letter was sent to the superintendent, or
the designated coordinator for the workshop, and a Workshop
Decision Questionnaire was sent to everyone who had received
the initial information from the researchers. If a questionnaire
was not returned within two weeks, a follow-up questionnaire
was sent. The questionnaire was an 18-item instrument
designed to measure the decision-making processes that led to
the workshop decision.

The workshop

The hospitals that agreed to the workshop were given a one-
day presentation, complete with slides, movies, and group
discussion. The audience usually comprised a broad base of
hospital staff and a sprinkling of community mental health
professionals. Participation was limited by mutual agreement to
a group of 25 or fewer people. The three-hour morning
session was a didactic presentation of the Community Lodge
program, covering the underlying basic assumptions, the
history and evaluation of the program, and some of the details
about implementation. The presentation was liberally spiced
with anecdotes about the prototype Lodge that had been established in the 1960s. The consultant showed a series of slides
and memorabilia from the first program, and also directed
attention to outcome data in terms of community tenure, cost,
and post-hospital employment. A movie depicting an ongoing
program in Minnesota was shown. To cap the morning session,
the audience was involved in a lengthy question and answer
session about the program.

The audience for the morning session was usually larger
than the one for the afternoon meeting. Many of the people
attending the morning session had only some casual interest or
curiosity about the program, and they often had little intention
or authority to implement the program in their unit. The
afternoon group, while sometimes smaller in number, usually
consisted of people who could conceivably set up the program,
and who might have some interest in doing so. Based on
previous workshop training experiences, the afternoon participants were therefore given an opportunity to discuss some
of the more tangible issues involved in actual implementation.
The audience was divided into several smaller groups which

met independently and discussed a consultant-initiated agenda. The topics were such logistical issues as funding, staffing, patient preparation, and finding a residence. During the small group deliberations, the consultant drifted from one group to another and functioned as a "resource person" and a group process facilitator as-needed. At the end of the day, the groups reconvened in a plenary session and compared notes on the conclusions reached. A five-page Workshop Effectiveness Questionnaire was distributed at this time.

Implementation decision

Two weeks after the workshop, the consultant wrote to the designated hospital contact person for a decision about receiving further Lodge consultation. Sometimes staff made an immediate decision; more frequently, they asked for additional time to make a decision, which led to subsequent follow-up contacts. A few hospitals received numerous calls before the decision was finally made. This was a typical negative decision:

> While we were interested and stimulated by your workshop held here in April, we do not feel it advisable to commit this hospital to a Community Lodge program at this time. We are in the process of considerable change which involves a large effort from many persons within the hospital and need to avoid becoming over-extended at this point in time. As we mentioned in our conversation during your visit, we may be in a position to consider a small group ward and community lodge program in the future, but are not able to make an immediate commitment now. Thank you for your interest and your interesting presentation.

The consultation services were also offered by letter to hospitals that had not initially accepted the workshop offer.
Of the 80 hospitals that received the workshop, 30 agreed to accept the first consultation and to attempt implementation of the innovation. In addition, one hospital that had not accepted the workshop at the time of initial contact, ultimately decided to opt for consultation services. This yielded an N of 31 hospitals that decided to attempt implementation. This group formed the sample for Phase II experiment.
In table 3.1 below are listed - in order of frequency - the most common reasons given by decision makers for rejecting the innovation. Clearly they run the gamut, with resource availability (e.g., money and staff) high on the list.

Table 3.1. Factors Affecting a Decision
to Reject the Innovation

1. No money
2. Lack of interest in the innovation
3. No staff to implement
4. Not a current priority
5. Inappropriate patient population
6. Negative administrative pressure
7. Negative community receptivity
8. Organizational restructuring precludes adoption
9. Already doing it
10. General inability to implement anything new
11. The philosophy of the innovation is incongruous with organizational values.
12. Local economic situation
13. General organizational constraints
14. The consultants were disliked
15. Legal restrictions preclude adoption
16. Disbelief in the data presented
17. No housing for patients in the community
18. Lack of information

When a decision was made by the institution, a Consultation Decision Questionnaire was mailed out to any person the researchers had communicated with at the hospital at any time. Similar to the Workshop Decision Questionnaire given out earlier, this 18-item questionnaire assessed the consultation decision process.

Experimental Manipulations

As indicated above, and as depicted in figure 3.1, the Phase I experiment involved the manipulation of three factors: Few/ Many initial contacts; High/Low Group Enhancement of discussion and interaction; and Staff/Administrator/Staff and Administrator involvement in decision making. What follows is a further elaboration of, and rationale for, these manipulations.

Few/many condition

The Few/Many staff contact dimension was a simple manipulation involving the number of staff who initially received information about the innovation, and who would consequently be involved in relevant decisions. During the initial phone call to the hospital, superintendents were asked to provide the researchers with the names of either six staff, for the Many condition, or two staff for the Few condition. The researchers

contacted the staff named and provided them with information
about the innovation. The intent was to involve them in
subsequent decision making.

The manipulation was not only an attempt to alter the
decision-making structure by involving more people than usual,
it was also an attempt to alter decision-making processes. As
we have frequently indicated, the decision-making process in
bureaucratic organizations often works against innovation
adoption. The typical unilateral decision making found in
complex organizations functions to screen out inputs for
change. The administrator of a public service bureaucracy
can be an effective "gatekeeper" who bars innovations from the
system. By involving six additional people (the Many condition), the researchers hoped to alter this process and
structure in order to preclude unilateral blockages to innovation. Involving additional people in the discussion could
result in more discussion, the introduction of more divergent
points of view, and the interaction of more people with varied
interests and experience. The Few condition was meant to
represent an analog to the usual decision-making process and
mode of discussion. However, as will be discussed in chapter
4, there is some question whether the Few condition actually
approximated unilateral decision making.

Level of staff condition

The level of staff dimension was almost purely a structural
manipulation. This dimension was designed to expand the
decision-making process to include people with a variety of
role and job functions. In mental hospitals, as in many
bureaucratic organizations, the administrative group often
makes decisions and hands them down to line staff. Several
responses to an open-ended questionnaire item indicate that

> Although one would immediately receive the
> impression that (our hospital) operates under a
> democratic system, this observation is false. The
> line staff has really very little to do with the
> development or implementation of programs. (Social
> Worker at Peaceful State Hospital)
> First, let me say that I don't know how the
> decision was made to implement the program at our
> hospital. I doubt if most of the peons do. What I
> write is pure conjecture, speculation, and/or
> occasional rumor. (Is there not a state policy that
> suggests that "higher-ups" should assist the
> peasants in maintaining their present level of
> ignorance?). (Nurse at Serene State Hospital)

This structural manipulation, like the Few/Many condition, was an attempt to alter the decision-making process by giving line staff an opportunity to become more involved in decisions. As indicated, our hypothesis was that the involvement of line staff would broaden the decision-making base, and result in a greater likelihood of a decision to implement the innovation. For purposes of the manipulation, "Staff" were defined as ward or unit administrators, and "Administrators" were defined as chiefs of service, medical directors, and the like. Obviously, both groups had administrative duties, but "Staff" were more intimately involved in direct service functions and patient care.

Group enhancement manipulation

This was a rather complex process manipulation designed to alter the intensity, amount, and frequency of group discussion and interaction. Specific group enhancement activities were used throughout Phase I, and the reader is advised to refer to table 3.2 to clarify the prose description that follows.

The first group enhancement manipulation occurred immediately after initial phone calls to the staff whose names had been obtained from the superintendent. The subjects in the High Group Enhancement hospitals were sent a letter suggesting that they talk and meet with the other staff who had received information about the innovation, as follows (emphasis added):

> We are also contacting a number of other members of the staff at your hospital. You will find their names below . Why not talk this matter over with some of them and come to a decision about whether this workshop would be helpful or not? Thus far, much of our communication with your hospital has been with the superintendent, who has functioned as a liaison. However, as we already mentioned to him, consideration of such a program requires maximum staff involvement. Your hospital might want to select a "contact person" who might coordinate your deliberations, and in the future all of our communication would be with him or her. We would like to have a decision about the workshop as soon as possible, but in any case, we will be contacting your hospital again in two weeks to determine your interest.

In contrast, the Low Group Enhancement letters made no suggestion that the staff should get in touch with each other, and in fact reinforced the traditional hierarchical structure, with the superintendent as nominal head.

Table 3.2.   Enhancing Group Decision Making:
One of Three Treatment Conditions.

Enhancing Group Decision Process   Not Enhancing Group Decision Process

Part I.   Persuading Hospitals
to Accept Workshop
Offers

Enhancing Group Decision Process	Not Enhancing Group Decision Process
1. Contact superintendent	1. Contact superintendent
2. Contact staff Suggest staff discuss workshop among themselves (names of all staff contacted enclosed) and select a leader to coordinate deliberations.	2. Contact staff
3. Carbon copies of letters sent to staff mailed to superintendent.	3. Carbon copies of letters sent to staff mailed to superintendent.
4. Contact asked for workshop decision Again, suggest staff discuss workshop offer.	4. Contact asked for workshop decision.

Part II.   Preparation for the Workshop

1. Sent brochure and letter to workshop participants. Suggest participants form a planning group, elect officers and select a group name.	1. Sent brochure and letter to workshop participants.

Part III: Implementing the Workshop

1. Workshop a. Group asked to select leader and group name. b. Leader asked to facilitate afternoon session. c. Group asked to plan future meeting to discuss program. d. Group photographed.	1. Workshop

Part IV. Post Workshop Activities

1. Leader received letter asking for decision.	1. Leader received letter asking for decision.
2. Leader received workshop certificate and photos to distribute to participants.	

In the High Group Enhancement condition, the researchers also sent the contacts <u>carbon copies</u> of all their correspondence with the superintendent. This was to ensure that the staff were maximally informed of, and it was hoped, included in, the discussion with the superintendent concerning the decision to hold the workshop. The superintendents in both high and low group enhancement conditions received a letter informing them that the researchers had contacted their staff, with a carbon copy of the letter that had been sent to their staff.

When the researchers were notified of a hospital's decision regarding the workshop, they sent a letter of acknowledgment to the superintendent or the designated decision maker. In addition, in the high group enhancement condition, a carbon copy was sent to the other staff contacts. Staff learned of the decision immediately.

From anecdotal reports, the researchers learned that on several occasions these small procedures resulted in the staff's appealing a superintendent's unilateral decision. In one instance, staff learned of a "no" decision by the superintendent from a carbon copy of the letter sent to him. The staff group then met and decided to request a meeting with the superintendent to inform him that staff were <u>very</u> interested in the Lodge program, and wanted to learn more about it. The superintendent was subsequently persuaded to change the decision, and the introductory workshop was held.

The enhancement of participative processes did not always work in favor of the researchers. In one instance, with circumstances almost identical to the above incident, the superintendent was persuaded by the staff to change his affirmative decision to a negative one.

The second major group enhancement manipulations took place after the workshop presentation offer was accepted. The workshop consultant set a workshop date, requested the necessary audio-visual equipment, and asked for a list of the workshop participants. A packet was then mailed to all the names on the list.

Those participants whose hospitals were in the Low Group Enhancement condition received the following short cover letter:

> Enclosed you will find a brochure describing the Hospital-Community Treatment Program. This program will be discussed in some detail at the workshop on __[date]__ . We are looking forward to seeing you at that time.

However, those staff whose hospitals were in the High Group Enhancement condition received a very different letter designed to facilitate their building a participative group, that would at least temporarily alter decision-making processes within the organization (emphasis added):

It might be helpful to give you an overview of the kinds of activities in which we have been engaged. Our research group has been involved in diffusing information about the Hospital-Community Treatment Program for several years. We have worked with dozens of hospitals throughout the nation, and have had many successful implementation efforts. We have gathered research data to ascertain the roadblocks which seem to hinder the implementation of the Hospital-Community Treatment Program. One of the most important factors is the degree to which the hospital has a group of staff who are able to work together in a coordinated, collaborative manner. In other words, there must be a real sense of "groupness" among hospital staff in order to muster the effort needed for implementing the program.

All of this has implications for the kind of activity staff at your hospital might wish to engage in prior to our workshop, in order to enhance the workshop experience. For example, in several hospitals that we have visited, workshop participants, prior to our coming, have formed an ad hoc community treatment group. Some, in fact, have given themselves names, and elected tentative officers. If such an ad hoc group is formed in your hospital, one of the activities it might consider is problem-solving around its own methods or procedures of interaction. Thus, an ad hoc group must decide when meetings are to be held, how people will interact in meetings, how decisions will be reached, etc. If your group becomes so motivated it is important to initiate this process relatively soon. We have included a list of workshop participants to help you toward this end.

Once again, all these activities will be, by necessity, voluntary at your institution. We would like to re-emphasize that our experience over the past several years has shown that some preparatory activity on the part of hospitals is desirable to enhance the workshop experience.

Here, the researchers were attempting to start some group discussion prior to the arrival of the consultant for the workshop. To facilitate this further, the following postscript was added:

P.S.   Our communications indicate that the following
individuals have tentatively agreed to attend
the workshop.   These are the people who
should be getting together for the pre-
workshop activities described above.

This was followed by a list of names of the participants.
     The third set of group enhancement manipulations took
place at the workshop itself.   After the morning portion of the
workshop, and just prior to breaking for lunch, the consultant
asked the participants in the High Group Enhancement condition to elect a group leader who would moderate the discussion
session for the rest of the day.   The leader's first task was to
direct the group in choosing a group name for itself and in
deciding where to go for lunch.   The consultant told the
group that this was a way to encourage the participants to
think of themselves as an "ad hoc decision group" rather than
as just an audience.   The consultant spent the rest of the day
observing the process and offering assistance when needed.
In the Low Group Enhancement condition, no such group
decision making was fostered, and the consultant rather than
someone from the group moderated the afternoon session.
     At the close of the workshop, one of the more unusual
Group Enhancement manipulations was undertaken.   Participants from hospitals in the High Group Enhancement condition
were asked to pose for a group photograph.   The consultant
then assured everyone that they would receive a copy of the
group photo (see figure 3.3) and a certificate recognizing
their participation in the workshop (see figure 3.4).

Fig. 3.3.   Group photo.

Michigan State University

awards this certificate of accomplishment to

in recognition of participation in

MSU-NIMH Innovation Diffusion Project

Hospital-Community Treatment Workshop

—— *day of* ——, 19——

_____
Workshop Director

A Continuing Education Program

Fig. 3.4. Workshop certificate.

52

Despite some initial trepidation, the responses to the request for a photo were mostly positive. It seems that many people have fond memories of similar pictures taken in kindergarten and grammar school. During Phase II of the project, the consultants often saw the photos prominently displayed at hospitals that agreed to subsequent consultations. In fact, on a few occasions when people mistakenly did not receive their photo and group certificate, they wrote the researchers asking for a copy.

Of course, staff at some hospitals responded negatively to the High Group Enhancement manipulations. One such response accompanied a subsequent letter to the research team:

> There was another related point which proved bothersome to a few. These few had the feeling that they were "in some sort of crude social psychology experiment." This feeling was doubtlessly elicited in part by being given the task of selecting a group name, a group leader, and by having the group photo taken. The manipulation to some felt like an aunt's setting you up on a blind date with a nice girl.

Two weeks after the workshop, the consultant wrote a letter to the designated hospital contact for a decision on receiving further Lodge consultation. Certificates and individual copies of the group photo were enclosed.

Anecdotal evidence uncovered later did indicate that the High Group Enhancement manipulations had definite effects on organizational processes. At one hospital which was in the condition, a unit psychiatrist formed a formal committee to discuss implementing the program. (This was explicitly suggested by the consultant at the workshop.) The committee members proposed that the Lodge be incorporated into the hospital's residential treatment program plan, which was itself still in the formative stages, and even started looking for appropriate patients. Unfortunately, when the committee informed the hospital's Assistant Director of its plans, he said the program wouldn't work and ordered the committee to disband and halt its planning activities.

Instruments

The three formal instruments used for the Phase I experiment were the Workshop Decision Questionnaire, the Workshop Effectiveness Questionnaire, and the Consultation Decision Questionnaire. The content and scale composition of each of the questionnaires is described below.

Workshop decision questionnaire

The Workshop Decision Questionnaire was sent to all persons
with whom the researchers had contact prior to the decision to
accept or reject the offer of a workshop presentation. Usually, this was either the superintendent and two others in the
Few condition, or the superintendent and six others in the
Many condition. It was an 18-item instrument, the primary
function of which was to assess changes in organizational
processes and interaction. It included such items as who was
involved in the decision, how much influence different people
had on the decision, how much discussion took place, to what
extent the respondent was satisfied with the decision, and the
like. Most of the items were structured as Likert-type
measures with four or five point response options.

Test-retest reliabilities were calculated for each of the 18
items during piloting. The average reliability was .90 or
better. A cluster analysis of the items revealed that all 18
items were part of a single dimension, which was subsequently
labeled the Participative I scale. The internal consistency, as
measured by Cronbach's alpha, was .83.

Workshop effectiveness questionnaire

At the conclusion of the workshop presentation, a 39-item
questionnaire was distributed to all workshop participants.
Since the workshop experience was the most intensive aspect
of the Phase I experiment, several domains of measurement
were sampled in the selection of questionnaire items. It should
be pointed out that because of the nature of the experiment, it
was impossible to do extensive pretesting of the questionnaire
and, as a result, the scales were developed using a combination of rational and empirical scale constructions.

One set of items was based partially on AVICTORY concepts, which have been developed by Davis (1973) to account
for an organization's readiness to change. AVICTORY stands
for: abilities (A); values (V); ideas (I); circumstances (C);
timing (T); obligations (O); resistances (R); and yield (Y).
Because of the considerable literature on the characteristics of
adopters and non-adopters (e.g., Rogers and Shoemaker,
1971), additional items focuses on cosmopolitism and demographics of the participants. Finally, several items were
specific to the Lodge innovation, and attitudes towards, and
perception of, the content presented in the workshop. The
average test-retest reliability for all items was .90 or greater.

Cluster analysis of the 39 items revealed five clusters
that roughly corresponded to the rational domains described
above. The first cluster was an acceptance of the philosophy
of the program (Philosophical Congruity, α = .89) and included
such items as a belief that patients can control their living

situation, a belief that they can develop a business, and a belief that they can be responsible for their own medication. The second cluster was an Organizational Tenure scale (α = .67) and included age, how long the person had worked there, and the number of different organizations the person had previously worked for. The third cluster captured perceptions that the Lodge was different from other mental health programs (α = .65). Items asked if the respondent believed that the Lodge and Hospital Small Group Ward programs were different from existing hospital programs. This was labeled Program Distinctiveness. The fourth cluster was an Organizational Readiness for Change scale (α = .77), and the items dealt with hospital resistance and whether or not such programs were high priority for the hospital. The fifth cluster was a Staff Readiness for Change cluster (α = .73). It included items that assessed the degree to which staff wanted to adopt, whether the timing was right, and whether staff had the time to start such a program. The latter two scales were basically what resulted after putting the ostensibly multidimensional aspects of the AVICTORY format (Davis, 1973) through a data reduction procedure.

For subsequent analysis of the data, cluster scores were computed for each of the cluster dimensions for every respondent. These scores were unweighted composites of the items in each cluster with the highest factor loading. Since the cluster analysis employed was an oblique solution, the derived scales were not independent. The correlations between the factor domains ranged from -.07 to .64, with an average of .23. However, since each of the five dimensions seemed to have distinct conceptual importance, they were analyzed subsequently as separate indices or scales.

Consultation Decision Questionnaire

When the consultation decision was made (see p. 43) a questionnaire was mailed to all the people at the hospital with whom the researchers had communicated up to this point. This was an 18-item questionnaire similar to the Workshop Decision Questionnaire but assessing the consultation decision process. The questionnaire asked who was involved in the decision, how much discussion took place, whether or not the respondent was satisfied with the decision, and so on.

A cluster analysis of the 18 items revealed that there were two clusters, highly related to one another. The first was a Participation II cluster (α = .89), which included such items as the amount of group discussion, degree of personal involvement in the decision, and satisfaction with the decision. The second cluster was a Social Influence cluster (α = .87), and included items that tapped the social status of the decision makers, the social status of those most talked to, and the

perceived influence that others may have had. The thrust of
the items was to indicate the extent to which decision making
was being broadened across disciplines and organizational
units. The correlation between the two clusters was .61.
Although this was quite high, it was felt that a compelling
case could be made for looking at these two slightly different
measures of participation in subsequent analyses.

Using procedures described above, cluster scores on
these two dimensions were also assigned to all respondents,
and were used in comparative and associative analyses.

Table 3.3 below lists each of the scales measured during
the Phase I experiment, and the timing of each.

The dependent measure: decisions for innovation

The Phase I intervention was, or course, ultimately designed
to move the sample of hospitals toward implementation of the
innovation. As such, there were two choice points embedded
in the process that functioned as indices of change, or
dependent variables.

One dichotomous choice was whether or not the hospital
wanted to be exposed to a workshop decision (Workshop Decision). A second choice - subsequent to the workshop - was
whether or not staff at the hospital wanted to receive consultation to aid them in implementation of the program (Consultation Decision). These two yes-no data points will be used in
subsequent comparative analyses as the principal dependent
variables of the Phase I experiment.

IMPLEMENTING THE INNOVATION: THE PHASE II EXPERIMENT

Once a hospital had agreed to attempt implementation of the
Lodge, Phase II of the research began. As described above,
Phase I was a relatively brief and transitory intervention
designed ideally to enhance a hospital's likelihood of initiating
implementation of the innovation. Phase II, in contrast,
addressed more persistent procedures and structures in the
organization, and in particular in the adopting unit, which
might obstruct the adoption of the innovation. Implementation
is a longitudinal process which requires sundry tactics to
maximize success. The hypothesis of the second experiment
was that through the use of organization development techniques a cohesive, task-oriented group could be set up, the
effectiveness of that implementing group would be enhanced,
and the degree of implementation would be increased accordingly.

Table 3.3. Phase I Instrumentation

Time	Questionnaire	Scales
0 – Initial Contact		
1 – 24 days	Workshop Decision Questionnaire	Participation I
2 – 66 days	Workshop Effectiveness Questionnaire	Philosophical Congruity Organizational Tenure Program Distinctiveness Organizational Readiness for Change Staff Readiness for Change
3 – 211 days	Consultation Decision Questionnaire	Participation II Social Influence

A viable group is vital to the establishment of a social innovation into an organization. Change leads to uncertainty about roles, authority, and what exactly one is doing, and the adopting group needs to have the internal flexibility and open communication to cope with these events. The Lodge program in particular produced a fair amount of uncertainty during implementation. What used to be a staff decision became the patients' responsibility. Democratic decision making needed to replace the typical unilateral decision making by the head nurse, psychiatrist, or ward chief. Such jobs as searching for funding, and finding resident employment and resident housing in the community, often alien tasks to hospital staff, became top priority items for successful implementation.

While the adopting group is working hard to implement the program, it also has to resist those pressures to preserve the existing order. A cohesive, supportive, task-oriented group is better equipped to withstand those pressures and creatively solve complex implementation problems. More specifically, this involves the group developing an organization structure which allows for the development and continuance of an innovative program.

Experimental Design

The design for Phase II was a simple, two cell experiment. Hospitals that were volunteers for consultation from Phase I were randomly assigned to either a Task Consultation condition (control), or a Task Consultation supplemented with Organization Development activities condition (see figure 3.5). One of the three consultants was randomly assigned to each of the 31 hospitals, and that consultant worked with the hospital throughout Phase II.

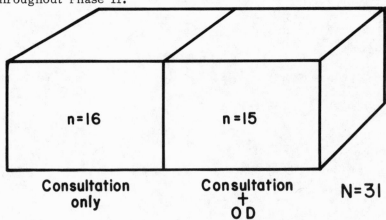

Fig. 3.5.   Phase II design: The OD experiment.

Sample

The sample for the Phase II experiment consisted of the 31 hospitals that responded affirmatively when a consultation decision was requested (see page 43). The geographic dispersion of the sample is demonstrated in figure 3.6.

Procedures: Task Consultation

As in previous discussions of experimental procedures, we present first activities common to both experimental conditions. In the Phase II, experiment these activities consisted of onsite consultation to assist hospitals in implementation tasks. This was labeled Task Consultation.

In order to assist staff in problem solving around these tasks, the research team offered hospitals four separate onsite consultations at the expense of the project. All of the four consultations lasted two days, with each subsequent consultation contingent upon certain demonstrated behavior commitments to the program, as shown in table 3.4.

Table 3.4.   Prerequisites for Receiving Consultations

Consultation I.   Identify a ward for the Small Group Ward Program. Select staff and identify possible patients.

Consultation II.   Administer the Small Group Ward for 60 days.

Consultation III.   Demonstrate a commitment for developing the Community Lodge by completing one of the following activities:

1. File for a non-profit corporation.

2. Locate a residence.

3. Develop a business or work.

4. Hire a Lodge coordinator.

Consultation IV.   Set a date for the move into the community.

When a hospital agreed to implement the program, it was under no legal obligation and could cease implementation activities at any time. The hospitals were only committed to receive the first consultation. As a prerequisite of Consultation I, the consultants asked only that staff from an adult psychiatric discharge ward who were interested in setting up the program attend the consultation, and that a potential ward or target group of patients be identified.

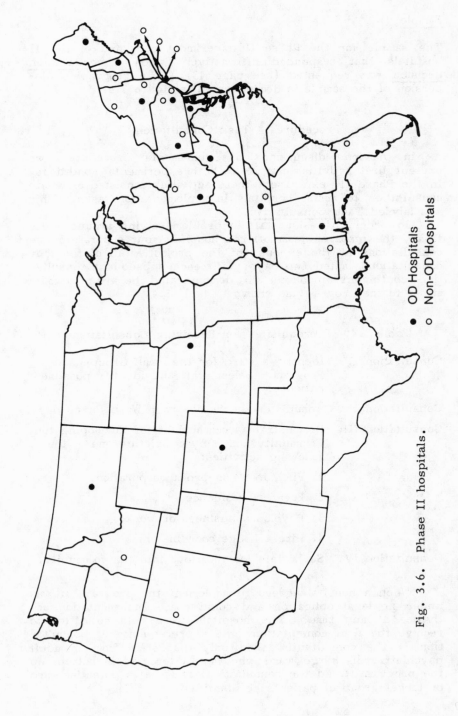

Fig. 3.6. Phase II hospitals.

● OD Hospitals
○ Non-OD Hospitals

Consultation I

Consultation I was a conceptual introduction to the program, and it focused on skillbuilding for the development of the hospital component of the innovation. Although much of this content had previously been covered in the workshop, it was quickly discovered in the early consultations that much had been forgotten during the interim. In addition, many participants in the consultation sessions, particularly lower status personnel such as aides, had never attended the previous workshop. Much of the consultation was therefore didactic and concentrated on the detailed tasks necessary for developing the in-hospital portion of the program, called the Small Group Ward (see Avellar, et al, 1978). The consultant and the staff worked together to tailor the program to fit the unique staff and hospital circumstances. At the conclusion of Consultation I, the consultant explained that the staff would have to start a Small Group Ward and run it for 60 days in order to receive Consultation II. The staff were also told that they could call the consultant collect if any questions or problems arose and that, in any case, members of the project staff would be in touch with them them by phone every 45 days.

Consultation II

The first day of Consultation II was devoted to troubleshooting problems related to the existing Small Group Ward. Staff were asked to identify problems that they were having with the program. The consultant listed them on a blackboard and later compiled them into three or four problem categories. The consultant focused on the identified problems during subsequent discussions and, when possible, provided staff with alternative solutions. Often, staff creatively developed their own solutions through discussion. Staff were also asked to give progress reports on performance of various tasks related to the Small Group Ward that had been discussed at Consultation I. The second day of Consultation II was devoted to introducing the community-based component of the program, the Community Lodge. This part of the consultation focused on plans for establishing the program in the community, including such things as forming a legal entity, identifying funding sources, finding suitable housing, etc. (see Avellar, et al., 1978). Staff were also given a list of criteria to fulfill in order to receive Consultation III.

Consultation III

This consultation was a follow-up on the planning and implementation of community component of the program. Little new information was presented at the third consultation. A checklist, including all necessary tasks to be completed prior to moving the patients into the Lodge, was gone over during the consultation. The consultant often visited the proposed housing site for the Lodge with the hospital staff.

Consultation IV

Consultation IV was held on the day the patients moved out of the hospital and into the Lodge. The move was usually a stressful event for the staff and patients. The consultant provided moral support and encouragement and helped the staff with any problems or tasks that may have been over-looked. Often the consultant became one of the movers, carried furniture, washed windows, checked plumbing, or drove Lodge members to the grocery store.

Experimental Manipulation

As indicated earlier, there were two consultation conditions: a Task Consultation condition and a Task Consultation plus Organization Development condition. The Organizational Development Package was designed to help the adopting group develop into a cohesive, supportive team capable of implementing the Community Lodge program. (It should be emphasized that the OD condition was a medley of disparate techniques. As such it was impossible to separate out the unique effect of each component. This remains so for subsequent research.) The OD exercises and feedback were purposefully tied to program implementation tasks; hospitals in both conditions received the same task information. In the Task Consultation condition, the consultant extended the task presentation to fill out both days of the visit. This was usually accomplished by asking task-related questions, eliciting discussion of the topics in more detail, and occasionally by having more breaks. In the Task Consultation plus Organization Development condition, the consultant presented the Organization Development exercises during the last several hours of the second day of consultation. The consultants used a variety of exercises designed to tap into different aspects of organization processes.

Survey feedback

The first OD exercise employed a modified version of the Survey Feedback Questionnaire (Taylor and Bowers, 1972), designed to gather data about the organization and then feed it back to the group for discussion. The survey feedback questionnaire is a set of items scorable into leadership, organizational climate, group satisfaction, and group climate scales.

The consultant distributed the questionnaire to the group at the end of the first day of the consultation. Data from the questionnaires were tallied during the evening of the first day, and the results were presented to the group the next day on a Survey Feedback Profile (see figure 3.7). The purpose of the Survey Feedback Questionnaire was to give staff some empirical information about how their organization might be hindering or supporting the development of the innovation. The group discussed the problems and tried to develop strategies for solving them.

The Survey Feedback inevitably revealed little administrative and interdepartmental support. The consultant usually pointed out that a Lodge program rarely received enthusiastic administrative support and the best that an adopting group could initially hope for was permission to pursue program development. The consultant tried to convince staff that minimal administrative support didn't necessarily mean that the program couldn't work, but that the problem would need ongoing attention.

The Survey Feedback Questionnaire was also administered at Consultation II. Often the problems of administrative support remained unchanged, but satisfaction, group process, and goal emphasis became more positive.

Team development

The second exercise was called Team Development. This intervention was designed to focus on the group's structure as a cohesive team. The exercise attempted to get the group to focus on the internal process of the actual functioning of their group. The group discussed and made decisions on issues of leadership, meetings, group process, group structure, external and internal communications, and assignment of task responsibilities. The group leader, rather than the consultant, led this exercise, and the consultant clarified the exercise for the group and answered questions that arose. Table 3.5 lists the topics and issues discussed.

Role clarification

The third exercise, Role Clarification, was intended to help individual staff members give themselves an identity unique to the task of implementing the program. The exercise focused on two core problem areas. The first area was the team members' need to develop an understanding of the purpose of each staff position in the hospital program; for example: why is the position needed? and what will the position contribute to the implementation of the program? The second area of focus was the need for role interdependence, that is, how each member's role depends upon and relates to another member's

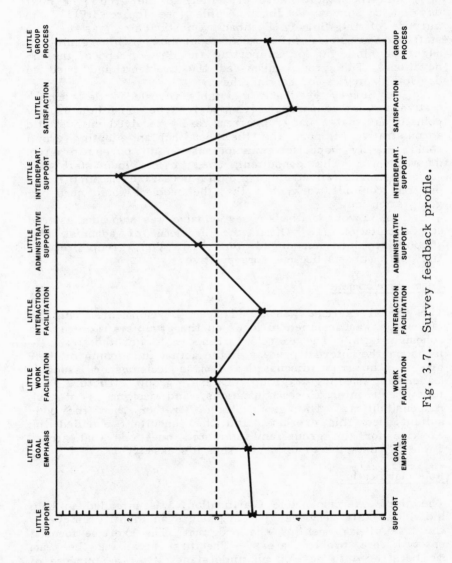

Fig. 3.7. Survey feedback profile.

Table 3.5.   Team Development Issues.

STRUCTURE

Issues: Looking over the task list, how does the group propose to handle these tasks?   Will committees or sub-committees be used?   Will the committees operate independently and autonomously or will they have to bring everything back to the group for final approval?

ASSIGNING OF TASKS

Issues: Who is going to be responsible for each of these tasks?   If committees are to be utilized, select a committee chairperson and the committee members to be responsible for each task.

LEADERSHIP

Issues: Will the Small Group Ward Planning Team become the Lodge Planning team?   Who will be the leader or coordinator of the Lodge Planning Team?

MEMBERSHIP

Issues: Is someone going to be a member of the Lodge Planning Team who is not already a member of the Small Group Ward Planning Team?   Is he/she here?   Is there anyone else who has expressed a willingness to help with the program that has not been asked to join?

PROCESS

Issues: Now that you are moving towards Lodge adoption will there be an opportunity for Small Group Ward Planning and Lodge Planning Staff to meet regularly?   If not, will there be a weekly executive meeting between the team leader or co-ordinator and the committee chairpersons and bi-weekly or monthly planning team meetings?

PROCEDURES

Issues: What will be the frequency and length of these meetings?   How will people be informed about the forthcoming meetings?   Will agendas be circulated ahead of time?   What will be the time and place of meetings?

EXTERNAL AND INTERNAL COMMUNICATION

Issues: What will be the circulation of group minutes and records?   Will special effort be made to communicate with important administrative persons within the hospital?

role. The exercises were intended to delineate explicitly the mutual obligations and task interdependence among staff and to minimize future misunderstandings and conflicts.

Onions and flowers

Since no OD intervention would be complete without some affect-oriented, sensitivity kinds of exercises, the authors used a fourth exercise called Onions and Flowers (Hanson, 1973). The exercise was designed to give group members a better understanding of the sociometry of their group. The exercise identified the underlying group leadership, and also identified the potential saboteurs of the implementation effort.

The technique required that everyone at the consultation identify on a slip of paper who they thought were the "most involved" (flower) or "least involved" (onion) in the meetings. In addition, the respondents were asked to estimate how many onions and/or flowers each of them would receive from the other members (see figure 3.8). This gave all the members the opportunity to determine whether the group's perception was consistent with their own. The number of onions and flowers was tallied, and a summary data sheet was constructed, showing the numbers of onions and flowers each person gave and received (see table 3.6 for an example). The exercise provided an opportunity, possibly a unique one, for members to discuss the cooperation or lack of cooperation among the group, and to find out the members' evaluation of their leader. The group suggested ways the least involved person could become more involved. Often the person who was minimally involved did not want to participate in the program. In these instances, it was necessary for the group to ask that person to transfer to another ward or program.

Often, members of the group felt personally threatened by the exercise, as it aroused feelings similar to the fear of being blackballed by a fraternity or sorority. At one consultation there was open rebellion. The nursing staff was clearly a blocking force whenever there was any discussion about implementing the program in the hospital. For example, whenever someone suggested a solution to an implementation problem, a nurse would say the nurses couldn't or wouldn't go along with it. By the time the Onions and Flowers exercise was presented, it was clear who were the onions at that hospital. However, before the consultant could discuss the results, the entire nursing team stood up and left the consultation.

Group picture

The fifth exercise was called the "group picture" (Hanson, 1973). The purpose of this exercise was to enable team mem-

Name _____
Give two flowers to whomever you felt was most involved in the
task group. You may give two flowers to the same person if
you felt their influence was outstanding. You can also give
flowers to yourself.
1.
2. _____

Give an onion to whomever you felt was least involved in the
task group. You may give yourself an onion, but please do
not use this as a way to avoid giving an onion to someone
else.

_____

Prediction of how many flowers and onions you will receive.

      Flowers _____
      Onions _____

Fig. 3.8.   Sociometric   instrument   (Onions   and   Flowers).

Table 3.6.   Onions and Flowers Summary.

Greg	Howard
1 flower	4 flowers
Dorothy	Susan
1 flower	3 flowers
	1 onion
Joe	Fred
1 flower	2 onions
	Mary
	2 flowers
	3 onions

In this situation the leadership probably revolves around
Howard and Susan, with opposition led by Mary and Fred. It
also appears that Mary has a leadership role in her own right.

bers to interact and observe group decision making and influence through a nonthreatening medium that was also atypical of everyday group interactions. Another purpose was to provide a fun exercise following a stress-producing exercise, Onions and Flowers. The group was divided into two or three smaller groups, and each subgroup was instructed to make a group picture, using a box of crayons and a sheet of blank newsprint. After a few minutes, the subgroups were asked to reflect on the interactions that led up to the completed pictures (e.g., how were the resources identified? Who was the most influential in deciding what to draw? Did anyone draw over another's picture?). After the discussion, the subgroups were instructed to pick the best picture. The discussions were often heated and generally ended in a deadlock - each group became polarized and was interested only in defending its own picture, without any consideration of actual artistic merit. The group picture was intended to reflect typical discussion in which everyone has a vested interest and no one wants to yield to the other group's wishes. Since discussion like this is common when an innovation is introduced into an organization, this exercise gave the group insights into how they functioned as a team in a setting of ambiguity and conflict.

The group picture exercise proved to be quite revealing and diagnostic in some settings. At one hospital, the staff refused to pick a best group picture. Instead, they taped all the pictures together and made a collage. The representatives then chose the collage as the best group picture. At another hospital, one subgroup tore its paper into as many pieces as there were members because the total group picture was not as good as each person's individual effort. Subsequent discussion revealed deep divisions and cliques within the staff group.

After this exercise was over, the group's behaviors often changed dramatically. Prior to the formation of subgroups, staff usually sat by their friends or by people who were in the same service (e.g., psychologists sat with psychologists, nurses sat with nurses, etc.). When the exercise was over, these previous groupings were disrupted. People often sat with their group picture subgroups and the physical distance between the groups increased. At later consultations, sometimes as much as a year later, staff would often still talk about the group picture exercise. A seemingly simple exercise often left a lasting memory, although its specific effect on actual innovation implementation is hard to determine, due to the obvious confounding of the various OD exercises.

Organization development at later consultations

Hospitals in the OD condition continued to receive organization development interventions after Consultation I. The Survey Feedback Questionnaire was re-administered, and the data were compared with earlier data to see if changes had occurred since the previous consultation. Similarly, role clarification exercises were tailored to reflect problems relevant to implementation of the hospital or community portion of the program. Roles changed as staff began planning for the community program component, but the issues involved were sufficiently common to warrant the use of a similar format. The team development exercises were employed and were also tailored to the changing program issues considered in the later consultations.

The OD interventions used at the third consultation were quite different from earlier exercises. It will be recalled that Consultation III was given only after staff had completed certain tasks related to Lodge adoption. The consultation was designed to orient the hospital or community staff to the tasks at hand. The main tool used, since no new task information was presented, was a checklist of principal tasks involved in setting up the hospital and community portions of the program. The items included such things as: where are you going to locate the house? have you arranged for furnishings? what kind of transporation will be available? have you arranged for transportation?

Subjects whose hospital was in the OD condition were asked if the tasks were done, and, if they were not completed, the consultant pressed the group to make someone responsible and give him or her a target date for completion of the task. The consultant attempted to help the program leader push for task completion and keep the group better organized and moving towards adoption. Everyone received a copy of the outline and was made fully aware of what needed to be done prior to the group leaving the hospital and moving into the community.

Instruments

The two instruments used for the second experiment were the Post Consultation Questionnaire and the Telephone Follow-up Questionnaire. The former questionnaire was designed to measure process changes; the latter questionnaire was designed to measure the dependent variable of implementation, or behavior that occurred in the second experiment.

Post consultation questionnaire

Sixty days after Consultation I, the Post Consultation Questionnaire was mailed out to all consultation participants. The questionnaire was designed to assess attitudes on five different scales. The first was an Internal-External Locus of Control scale (α= .91), which was adopted for use in an organizational setting by one of the researchers (Bond and Tornatzky, 1973). Items measured respondents' beliefs that they could influence hospital affairs and the decisions that affected them. Examples of items are: "The average staff person can have an influence in hospital decisions;" and "As far as hospital affairs are concerned, most of us are victims of forces we can neither understand nor control." The second scale measured Group Affect (α= .91). The items assessed the subjects' perceptions of the degree of affect at staff meetings. Sample items are: "Members often 'kid' each other and make jokes while doing serious group business;" and "Laughter and loud noise are common in our meetings." The third scale measured Group Process (α= .87), or the decision and discussion process at staff meetings. Among these items are: "Everyone at staff meetings gets a chance to express his/her opinion;" and "Decisions are made at these meetings only after each person had had a chance to speak." The fourth scale measured the Support (α= .89) the group believed it was getting from discipline chiefs and top management. Items which comprise this scale include: "The top management (superintendent, assistant superintendent, clinical director) in this hospital supports the Hospital-Community Treatment Program;" and "Persons in different professional groups (psychiatry, psychology, nursing, social work, rehabilitation, etc.) have cooperated to help set up the Hospital-Community Treatment Program." What is the range and mean of intercluster correlations?

Follow-up phone questionnaire

Implementation outcome was assessed by means of a six-page follow-up questionnaire, administered over the telephone. The consultants called the program leader at 45-day intervals, starting after Consultation I and concluding at the end of one year after the date of the first consultation. (Those hospitals still actively involved in implementation continued to receive follow-up calls for up to one additional year, though these calls were primarily of a consultative nature, and no data as such were gathered. The other, "nonimplementing" hospitals were quite happy to be rid of us after one year.) Two different series of questions were used: hospitals in the process of setting up a small group ward were questioned on items relevant to that task; hospitals involved in implementation of the Lodge were asked additional questions.

The phone calls served two purposes. The first purpose was to provide staff with consultative help, and the second was to provide the researchers with follow-up data on the hospital's progress toward implementation of the innovation. The interview was largely open-ended and directed to the designated hospital contact for the program. Information on implementation per se was obtained by use of checklists of related tasks. The interview also tapped staff satisfaction with the program's progress, and names of staff involved in program development. The telephone interview not only gave the researchers an opportunity to collect data, but also enabled them to answer questions or give advice on any problems the leader might be having with the program.

Sometimes the responses from the contacts were unexpected. At one hospital, the hospital contact said she was afraid to tell all that was on her mind. The contact said she feared that someone was listening in on her phone calls because she had been asked about comments she had made in confidence on the telephone by someone else in the hospital.

Since implementation of the innovation required the accomplishment of a number of easily identifiable steps (see table 3.7), this checklist information provided the raw data for an implementation score. The items were tallied, and an omnibus Degree of Implementation index was computed. Previous experience, and data, in implementing the ward and Lodge aspects of the innovation suggested the need for weighting the accomplishment of implementation tasks, based on the mean time necessary for completion of the two sets of tasks. Items specific to implementation of the small group ward were counted and divided by seven. If nothing was done, the hospital received a score of zero. If the hospital set up the small group ward (i.e., received Consultation II, since running the ward for 60 days was a condition for receiving this consultation), the Community Lodge checklist was additionally used. There were 26 items related to Lodge implementation. The items which had been completed were counted and multiplied by .0481, and this number was added to the samll group ward total above.

Although data were collected at 45-day intervals, scores were computed at 90, 180, 270, and 360-day intervals in order to simplify analysis and interpretation. Also, "1" was added to all the scores to facilitate later analysis. These computational procedures ultimately yielded a Degree of Implementation score that ranged from 1 to 3.25. The results of this four-year effort will be detailed in the following chapters.

Table 3.7.   Small Group Ward and Lodge Implementation
Checklist Follow-up Telephone Questionnaire

I.   Small Group Ward Tasks - Use Part I until Consultation II and do not use thereafter.

1.   Has a ward been selected?   ___Yes   ___No
2.   Have staff been assigned to work on the ward?   ___Yes   ___No
3.   Have patients been assigned to groups?   ___Yes   ___No
4.   Has a step-level-reward system been established?   ___Yes   ___No
5.   Have group work assignments been arranged?   ___Yes   ___No
6.   Has a daily ward schedule been developed?   ___Yes   ___No
7.   Have the necessary forms for the program been completed?   ___Yes   ___No

Sum "yes" responses on question 1-7 and divide by seven to compute change score.

II.   Lodge Tasks - Use Part II after Consultation II has taken place.

1.   Have residents met to discuss plans for the lodge?   ___Yes   ___No
2.   Have the residents made any decisions about their living arrangements
     in the lodge?   ___Yes   ___No
3.   Have decisions been made about assigning roles, such as cook, crew
     chief, etc., to Lodge members?   ___Yes   ___No
4.   Has anything been done about staff coverage in the Lodge?   ___Yes   ___No
5.   Has a Lodge coordinator been assigned?   ___Yes   ___No
6.   Has a system been established for the coordinator to communicate
     with the hospital staff?   ___Yes   ___No
7.   Has a building for the Lodge been found?   ___Yes   ___No
8.   Has financing for the housing been resolved?   ___Yes   ___No
9.   Have furnishings for the Lodge been obtained?   ___Yes   ___No
10. Have arrangements been made for residents to receive medication
     in the community?   ___Yes   ___No
11. Has a system been formulated for how food will be purchased and
     prepared?   ___Yes   ___No
12. Has a system been formulated for how laundry will be done?   ___Yes   ___No
13. Has a system for staff on-call coverage been developed for the
     hours that the coordinator is off duty?   ___Yes   ___No
14. Have arrangements been made for transportation?   ___Yes   ___No
15. Has a business been selected?   ___Yes   ___No
16. Has the Lodge coordinator been trained in that particular business?   ___Yes   ___No
17. Has any plan been made about how quality of work will be monitored?   ___Yes   ___No
18. Has the necessary equipment been obtained for the work?   ___Yes   ___No
19. Has insurance been secured?   ___Yes   ___No
20. Have bonding arrangements for the residents been made?   ___Yes   ___No
21. Has a decision been made about how the income from their work will be
     divided?   ___Yes   ___No
22. Will the residents work in crews?   ___Yes   ___No
23. Have the residents gone out on any actual jobs in the community?   ___Yes   ___No
24. Has a non-profit corporation or other legal entity been established?   ___Yes   ___No
25. Do you have a board?   ___Yes   ___No
26. Has a decision been reached on the legal status of the Lodge members?   ___Yes   ___No

Sum "yes" responses on Part II questions 1-26 and multiply by 0.481.

4 Participative Decision Making and Innovation

INTRODUCTION

The Phase I experiment was the first part of a multistage effort designed to achieve implementation of the Community Lodge innovation in a national sample of mental hospitals. An attempt was made, through experimental manipulations, to alter decision-making structures and processes that were hypothesized to be related to innovation adoption. Particular attention was focused on enhancing the participative decision-making climate within the organization by the use of several intervention tactics. The research design was a 3x2x2 factorial experiment constructed to test the causal relationships between participative decision making and related group processes, and decisions favorable to implementation of the Lodge innovation. By way of review, the hypotheses discussed below were directly tested by the three factors of the experimental design.

Breadth of Involvement in Decisions/ Hypothesis 1

Contacting several people, rather than a few, upon initiating interaction with an organization will increase the base for decision making, which will in turn increase the likelihood of decisions for innovation. The simple assumption here was that viable participation may simply be a function of the number of people involved. By precluding unilateral decision making at entry, it was hoped that some blockages to change would be removed. A Many versus Few experimental manipulation of number of initial contacts was employed. (The reader is referred to chap. 3, fig. 3.1, for a graph of the Phase I experiment).

Intensity of Involvement in Decisions/Hypothesis 2

If the nucleus of an adopting group of staff could be developed during the approach/persuasion interactions with the institutions, then a greater degree of ultimate adoption would be likely to be obtained. In short, if a greater intensity, frequency, and breadth of discussion and interaction could be facilitated, then decisions favorable to innovation should result. This was tested via High versus Low Group Enhancement experimental conditions.

Organizational Role of Decision-Makers/Hypothesis 3

Contacting line Staff, and personnel other than top level Administrators in the initial approach to the hospital should also alter the decision-making base. This, in turn, should yield a greater likelihood of decisions favorable to innovation. An implicit assumption was that the role and job function of organizational members are an important aspect of participation. This led to an experimental manipulation of the level of staff contacted (Staff versus Administrators versus a mixed group of Staff and Administrators).

In addition to these three main hypotheses that were tested by the experimental design, a number of other subsidiary questions were examined. For example, one commonly held belief is that positive attitudes toward an innovation should increase the likelihood of its adoption. This notion was examined via attitudinal data and correlational techniques. The acronym (defined in chap. 3) AVICTORY (Davis, 1973), has been used as a representation of various dimensions that ostensibly influence adoption, which are all aspects of general "readiness" for change. The research thus examined the relationship between "readiness" measures and innovation decisions.

Finally, data were also gathered on a host of other organizational process variables, archival measures, social milieu indices, and the like. What follows is a description of the data reduction and analysis procedures employed, and the results obtained.

PROCESS RESULTS

Introduction

Before presenting data on the three main hypotheses relating organizational process and, moreover, the experimental manipulations to adoption decisions, we will present results addressing a more fundamental question. Before we can examine the effects of the experiment on the principal dependent variables, we need to consider whether the manipulated factors, in fact, had their intended effect on intervening organizational processes and structures that impact on participative decision making. To this end, the effects of the treatment conditions on various attitudinal and decision-making processes within the hospitals, as measured by the three formal questionnaires, will be presented here.

Parenthetically it should be noted that the level of contacts condition and number of contacts condition both affected participative decision making, almost by definition (see pages 44 to 46). As the data presented below will show, we did, in fact, initially contact more people in the Many condition; we did contact staff in different job functions in the level of contacts condition. These were structural manipulations. From the perspective of a person viewing the interventions from outside the organization, the expansion of participation is "obvious." What remains to be seen, however, is their impact on felt participation by members of the organization.

Analytic considerations

In all of the ANOVA's (analyses of variance) to be reported on these questionnaire data, it should be noted that our design - for purposes of analyzing data from individuals - constituted a hospital within treatment cell nest. This had some deleterious impact on the error term that was used to test treatment main effects, particularly in those cases when the hospital factor was significant. Following procedures outlined by Winer (1971), a preliminary test was made of the nested hospital factor against the normal error term. If significant ($p < .05$ was used as a criterion significance level), the hospital factor was then used as the denominator for subsequent F ratios to test treatment effects, rather than the usual error term. This indeed became a conservative test. If the hospital was not significant, then a pooled error term was used. More on the methodological and conceptual importance of this issue will be presented below.

On the nature of process data

A legitimate view sees the nature of organizational innovation as a complex, unfolding process (Eveland, Rogers, and Klepper, 1977) rather than as a sequence of discrete events. As has been pointed out by Rogers (1975), "almost none" of the existing literature on innovation has studied stages and roles in the innovation process, particularly at the organizational level. In the current study an explicit attempt was made to capture the sequential nature of that process. To this end, during the Phase I experiment, questionnaire data were gathered at three points in time, each of which involved a significant set of events for the organization.

The Workshop Decision Questionnaire data were gathered from the initial contacts, on the average, 24 days after initial contact with the organization, and corresponded chronologically to the first innovation decision point. The Workshop Effectiveness Questionnaire was administered to all participants at the workshop 66 days after the first contact with the hospitals. The Consultation Decision Questionnaire data were gathered from all staff who had been in contact with the research team at the termination of the Phase I experiment, an average of 211 days after initial contact with the hospitals. This corresponded to the time period immediately after a hospital had decided for or against attempting implementation. The scales comprising these questionnaires have been presented in chapter 3. It was felt that these three time periods represented the most salient cross sections of organizational behavior during Phase I activities.

In presenting results on the three factors of the experimental design, we will therefore be presenting questionnaire data collected at each of these three time periods. Much of the criticism of using structured questionnaires to study the innovation process is that such procedures ostensibly fail to capture the richness of the phenomena included. By employing repeated cross-sectional structured measures in this study, we have hoped to combine richness and measurement rigor.

Breadth of Involvement - Many/Few Process Results

Two manipulation checks

As will be recalled from the above discussion, the Many-Few manipulation was intended as a structural manipulation, hopefully with the effect of offsetting the bureaucratic structure's tendency toward unilateral decision making.

To evaluate the effect of the experimental treatment, we should first determine the extent to which more people were involved at the initiation of our contacts and interactions with sample organizations. To this end, two separate analyses were performed. One was a simple count of the number of people who were contacted during initiation activities. Inspection of these means indicates highly significant differences ($t = -9.06$; $df = 106$; $p < .001$; $\bar{X}$ for many = 4.77; $\bar{X}$ for few = 1.91), confirming that significantly more persons were contacted in the Many condition than in the Few condition.

A second test of the effect of this structural manipulation was obtained by looking at the response rate data for the various questionnaires. An "index of continuity" was computed on the basis of the number of people who returned all three questionnaires. It can be construed as a measure of the breadth of decision making produced by the manipulation. Inspection of the means indicates a significant difference between the Many and Few conditions on this index (t = -2.59; df = 79; p .01); $\bar{X}$ for many = 1.21; $\bar{X}$ for few = .60), with more people returning questionnaires in the Many condition than in the Few condition.

From the above data, we can safely state that the manipulation did take place, at least in its structural manifestation. Now we will consider its impact on respondents' perception of felt participation, and related organizational processes.

Questionnaire results

As indicated above, three questionnaires were employed, at three distinct points in the participative decision-making intervention process. In Table 4.1 below is a summary of the Analyses-of-Variance results for these data.

As can be seen from Table 4.1, of the eight measurement scales represented on the three questionnaires, only one, Organizational Tenure, was significant (p < .005) for the Many-Few treatment. Interestingly enough, the nature of the difference here was that participants in the workshop on the Many condition tended to be younger, more vocationally mobile, and had less tenure in the current organization. To the extent that the Many-Few "structural" manipulation was attempting to change the decision-making mix, it appears to have been successful, as measured by this variable.

There is little evidence, however, that the perception of participative processes was altered much by the treatment, or in the expected direction. Neither the Participation I nor Participation II scales showed significant differences.

Two significant interactions were found that are noteworthy. There were significant interactions between the Few-Many condition and the Level of Staff condition on the Program Distinctiveness scale (F = 4.124; df = 2,72; p <.02) and on the Organizational Readiness for Change scale (F = 3.044; df = 2,72; p <.05), both of which involved data collected at the time of the workshop presentation.

What seems to be occurring in both these interactions (see figures 4.1 and 4.2) is that the effect of the Few versus Many manipulation seems to be moderated by whether the initial contact group is a mixture of Staff and Administrators, versus a group composed exclusively of Administrators, or exclusively of line Staff. If a mixed group is involved, it appears that

Table 4.1. Number of Contacts.

Time	Instrument and Scale	Results		
		F	p	df
T_1	**Workshop Decision Questionnaire**			
	Participation I	.738	ns	1, 72

Instrument and Scale	F	p	Few	Many	df
Workshop Effectiveness Questionnaire					
Philosophical Congruity	.018	ns			1, 72
Organizational Tenure	8.274	< .005	.0632	-.0844	1, 72
Program Distinctiveness	.086	ns			1, 72
Organization Readiness for Change	.713	ns			1, 72
Staff Readiness for Change	.737	ns			1, 72

T_2

Instrument and Scale	F	p	df
Consultation Decision Questionnaire			
Participation II	2.916	ns	1, 72
Social Influence	.137	ns	1, 72

the perceived incongruity or, as we have labeled it, Program
Distinctiveness of the innovation seems to become exacerbated
by broadening involvement in terms of numbers.   Not surprisingly, there is a correspondingly reduced perception of
Hospital Readiness for Change.   The effect of the Many
manipulation seems, in contrast, to be more "positive" with
unmixed groups of Staff, or Administrators, respectively.
One interpretation of these findings could be that the
forcing of discussion of an innovation across different organizational levels has the effect of intensifying and highlighting
the potential conflict and disruption associated with an innovation.   Perhaps different parties to the decision-making
process relative to an innovation need to be kept separated,
depending upon their role in the organization, and their
function in the process of implementation.

In summarizing the questionnaire data, it appears that the
structural Many-Few condition did expand the number, and
mixture, of participants in decision making relative to the
Lodge innovation.   However, in retrospect it may be that the
full impact of this type of treatment was attenuated by the
specific operations of this study.   Recent data (Stevens and
Tornatzky, 1979) an innovation dissemination study with a
sample of drug abuse treatment organizations would indicate
that the involvement of even one additional person in decision
making may break down a unilateral decision-making pattern.
In another study reported by Corbett and Guttinger (1977), a
comparison was made between a single administrator, versus
staff team, attendance at a technical assistance workshop.
Team participation markedly increased the likelihood of implementation of an educational innovation, even if only one
additional person was added to form the team.   Since we
involved at least three individuals (the superintendent and two
other staff) in our Few condition, perhaps we had already
overcome many of the deleterious effects of unilateralism, and
not performed a completely clean test of the hypothesis.

Subsidiary comparative analyses

In addition to the ANOVAs of the eight questionnaire-based
scales, a number of additional comparative analyses were
performed on various other data points.   These included
archival information, single items from the questionnaires which
did not fall into a factor domain, open-ended items which were
subjected to in-depth content analysis, and the like.   A total
of 22 such variables were subjected to either parametric or
nonparametric comparative analyses.   Obviously, because of
their possible dubious psychometric quality, and absolute
number, significant findings from the subsidiary analyses
ought to be considered suggestive rather than definitive.
Aside from the "manipulation check" data already cited, no

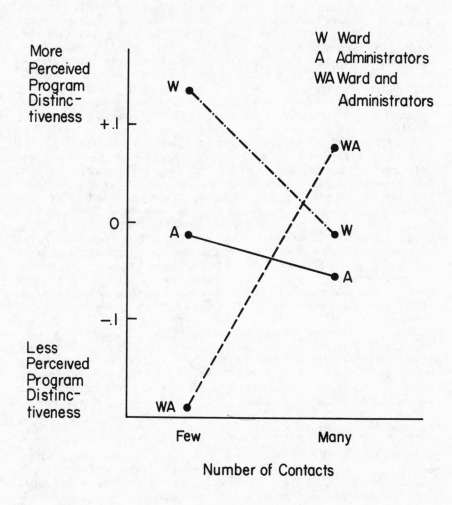

Fig. 4.1. Many-few by level of staff interaction for program distinctiveness.

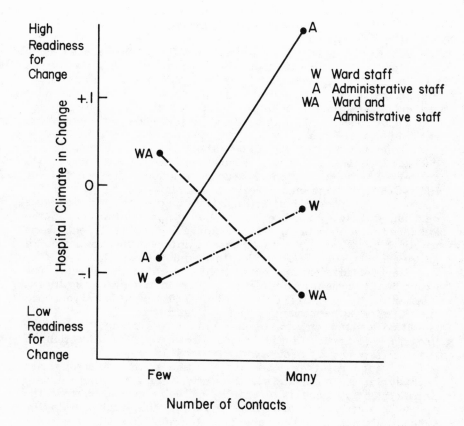

Fig. 4.2. Many-few by level of staff interaction for hospital readiness for change scale.

other significant differences were found between the Many and Few conditions on these variables.

Intensity of Involvement in Decisions/Group Enhancement Process Results

Inasmuch as this treatment was substantially a "process" oriented manipulation, we will look immediately at the questionnaire data. The overall intent of the High Group Enhancement treatment was to increase the amount, intensity, and frequency of participative decision making about the innovation. Table 4.2 presents the Analysis-of-Variance results for the eight questionnaire scales, at the three time periods respectively.

Questionnaire Results

Inspection of Table 4.2 indicates significant differences (F = 4.02; df = 1,72; p < .05) on the Participation I scale, which was administered immediately after the workshop decision. Inspection of the cell means further points out that the High Group Enhancement condition had produced a heightened degree of perceived participation and interaction, even this early in the process.

Consideration of the data subsequent to the consultation decision yields a picture similar to the results described above. The Participation II scale once again indicates that the High Group Enhancement treatment is signigicantly (F = 5.97; df = 1,72; p < .02) affecting the degree of participative decision making, as perceived by our respondents. Thus, the enhanced involvement and discussion observed at Time 1 seems to continue throughout the Phase I intervention, a period of approximately seven months for the typical hospital.

Several interesting interactions were found involving the group enhancement manipulation. For instance, a significant interaction (F = 3.61; df = 2,72; p < .05) was found between the Group Enhancement condition and the Level of Staff condition on perceptions of the uniqueness of the innovative program (Program Distinctiveness scale). The direction of these differences is depicted in figure 4.3.

It appears that when the initial contact persons are exclusively Administrators, the effect of the High Group Enhancement devices is to heighten their perception that the Lodge innovation is "different." To put this finding into the conceptual discussions of chapters 1 and 2, we might surmise that increased discussion and participation may be serving to increase felt uncertainty about innovation among administrators. In contrast, when the initial contacts involve line Staff - those closer to the logistical problems of implementation - the effect of enhanced discussion and participation is to reduce the perceived differences, or Program Distinctiveness, of the innovation. This finding has interesting implications for subsequent experimental studies of intervention techniques. It may mean that a contingency approach is called for, emphasizing participation and discussion at the level of the adopting unit, while at the same time trying to minimize discussion and feelings of impending threat among administrators.

Additionally, there was a significant (F = 3.390; df = 2,72; p < .04) Group Enhancement by Level of Staff condition on interaction on the social Influence scale. The High Group Enhancement manipulation seemed to increase the respondents' perception of influence for the Administrative group, and decrease the perception of influence for the Staff group. The effect on the mixed group seems moot. Figure 4.4 shows the interaction patterns.

Table 4.2. Group Enhancement.

Time	Instrument and Scale	Results				
		F	p	High	Low	df
T_1	Workshop Decision Questionnaire					
	Participation I	4.016	p < .049	.163	-.209	1, 72
T_2	Workshop Effectiveness Questionnaire	F	p			df
	Philosophical Congruity	.001	ns			1, 72
	Organizational Tenure	.756	ns			1, 72
	Program Distinctiveness	.030	ns			1, 72
	Organization Readiness for Change	.026	ns			1, 72
	Staff Readiness for Change	.116	ns			1, 72
T_3	Consultation Decision Questionnaire	F	p			df
	Participation II	5.967	p < .017	.0654	-.0986	1, 72
	Social Influence	.223	ns			

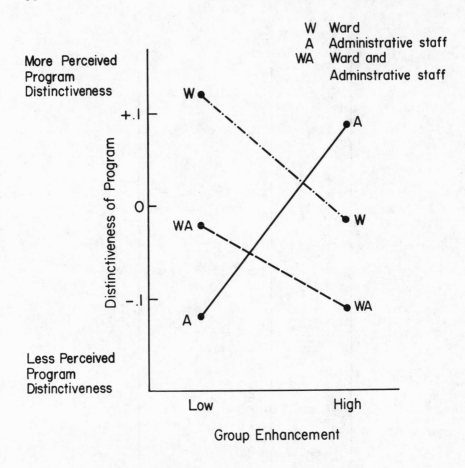

Fig. 4.3. Group enhancement by level of staff interaction for program distinctiveness scale.

The apparent nature of this group enhancement was to increase the influence of disparate disciplines. Since the "Administrators" in the Administrators only condition were primarily heads of disciplines (e.g., Psychiatry, Psychology, Social Work, and Nursing), and since the Social Influence scale primarily measures enhanced participation across disciplinary organizational units, the results make sense. The net sum of influence in the organization was increased. This findings is quite in keeping with the classical findings reported by Tannenbaum (1968) on organizational control structure.

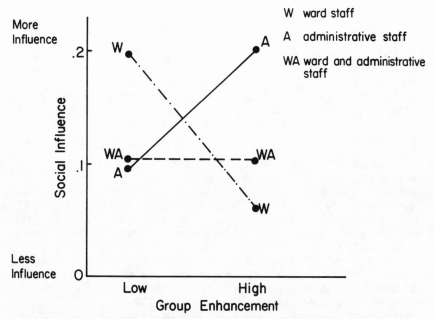

Fig. 4.4 Group enhancement by level of staff interaction for social influence scale.

Subsidiary analysis

Two findings from the comparative analyses of the archival and miscellaneous variables referred to above are also noteworthy. The status of the "contact person" - our liaison with the hospital - was constantly monitored throughout Phase I. Our data indicate that the status of this contact changed significantly downward as a result of the High Group Enhancement manipulation. Clearly a significant delegation of authority to line level staff is occurring ($F = 4.858$; df = 1,82; $p < .03$) for organizations in the high group enhancement condition. The mean score for the high group enhancement condition was 2.18; the mean for the low group enhancement condition was 1.73 (higher score indicates lower status rating).

A second finding is also relevant. Several questionnaire items enabled us to compute a measure of who was the "sociometric star," or recipient of significant amounts of communication from other staff at various stages of the innovation process. One index was obtained of the status of the "star" at the time of the workshop presentation. There is a significant downward delegation of participation that can be inferred ($F = 5.988$; df = 1,64; $p < .02$). The high group enhancement mean was 3.67, and the low group enhancement mean was 3.16 (higher score equals lower occupational status).

Organizational Role of Decision Makers/Level of Staff Process Results

Like the Many-Few manipulation, the Level of Staff represented an attempt to manipulate a "structural" organization variable. Prior to examining the effects of this condition on various indices of decision making, we examined the extent to which the condition was, in fact, implemented.

Two manipulation checks

One measure examined the functional role of respondents during our initial phone contacts. They did differ as a function of the Administrators/Staff/Administrators and Staff manipulation (F = 14.347; df = 2,93; p <.001). The means were as follows: Staff = 2.81; Administrators = 2.10; Staff and Administrators = 2.53 (higher score indicates lower occupational status).

A second, more indirect, index of the manipulation can be obtained by looking at the occupational status of the contact person at the time of the consultation decision. As described in chapter 3, the contact functioned as the hospital liaison to the research project. There were differences on this variable as a function of the manipulation, that approach significance (F = 2.654; df = 2,82; p < 1). The means were: Staff = 2.25; Administrators = 1.87; Staff and Administrators = 1.73 (higher score indicates lower occupational status).

Questionnaire results

The effect of the Level of Staff manipulation on the various measures of organizational processes and decision making can be captured quite succinctly. Aside from the significant interaction effects previously discussed (see pages 81 to 83), there were no significant effects of the manipulation as measured by the questionnaires. In addition, there were no effects discernible in other subsidiary analyses. The net effect of the manipulation on organizational processes was to moderate and alter the impact of the other experimental conditions.

EXPERIMENTAL CONDITIONS AND INNOVATION

Innovation Decisions

It will be recalled that the operationally-defined indices of innovation during the Phase I experiment were to be represented by the two choice points presented to organizations

Table 4.3. Level of Staff.

Time	Instrument and Scale	Results		
		F	p	df
T_1	Workshop Decision Questionnaire			
	Participation I	.077	ns	2, 72
T_2	Workshop Effectiveness Questionnaire	F	p	df
	Philosophical Congruity	.008	ns	2, 72
	Organizational Tenure	.159	ns	2, 72
	Program Distinctiveness	1.291	ns	2, 72
	Organization Readiness for Change	.961	ns	2, 72
	Staff Readiness for Change	1.801	ns	2, 72
T_3	Consultation Decision Questionnaire	F	p	df
	Participation II	1.803	ns	2, 72
	Social Influence	.898	ns	2, 72

during these intervention activities. The initial choice was whether or not the hospital wished to receive a workshop presentation. This was the workshop decision. The second choice was whether or not the hospital was willing to make a commitment to implement the innovation, and receive consultation technical assistance. This was the consultation decision. The three experimental conditions will now be compared as they relate to these innovation decision data.

Many-few condition

Tables 4.4 and 4.5 present data on the Workshop and Consultation decisions respectively, comparing the Many and Few conditions. As can be seen, neither of the comparisons approach customary levels of statistical significance. (Reflecting the discussion on page 40, 14 hospitals were eliminated from these and subsequent X^2 analyses. Since the superintendents refused to give members of the research team the requested names, the conditions were never implemented as planned. It should be noted, however, that the exclusion of these hospitals did not significantly alter the thrust of the general findings.)

Group enchancement conditions

Tables 4.6 and 4.7 present X^2 analyses comparing the High and Low Group Enhancement conditions on the Workshop and Consultation decisions, respectively. The tables indicate that the comparisons do not even remotely approach usual levels of significance.

Level of staff conditions

Tables 4.8 and 4.9 present comparisons between the three experimental conditions manipulated for this factor. As can be seen, there is a significant difference between conditions for the workshop decision ($p < .02$), which does not persist through the subsequent consultation decision.

Inspection of table 4.8 will reveal an interesting pattern of results. Apparently if ward staff are involved at all - either exclusively or in concert with administrators - there is a much higher probability of a positive decision being made about the workshop. For illustration, if we collapse the Ward and Ward Administration conditions together, we find that 91.5 percent of the hospitals in these conditions decided to receive a workshop, compared to only 68.6 percent of the hospitals in the Administration only condition. This is convincing evidence for both the existence of unilateral blockages to innovation and for the utility of a simple "structural" intervention tactic.

Table 4.4. Comparison of Many-Few Conditions
on Workshop Decision.

Workshop Decision	Number of Staff Contacted	
	Many	Few
Yes	37	41
No	8	8

x^2 = .035; ns; df = 1

Table 4.5. Comparison of Many-Few Conditions
on Consultation Decision.

Consultation Decision	Number of Staff Contacted	
	Many	Few
Yes	17	13
No	28	36

x^2 = 1.365; ns; df = 1

Table 4.6. Comparison of Group Enhancement Conditions
on Workshop Decision.

Workshop Decision	Group Enhancement	
	High	Low
Yes	35	43
No	9	7

x^2 = .689; ns; df = 1

Table 4.7. Comparison of Group Enhancement Conditions
on Consultation Decision.

Consultation Decision	Group Enhancement	
	High	Low
Yes	14	16
No	30	34

x^2 = .0004; ns; df = 1

Table 4.8. Comparison of Level of Staff Conditions on Workshop Decision.

Workshop Decision	Ward	Type of Staff Administration	Ward & Administration
Yes	29	24	25
No	2	11	3

$x^2 = 8.3843$; p < .02; df = 2

Table 4.9. Comparison of Level of Staff Conditions on Consultation Decision.

Consultation Decision	Ward	Type of Staff Administration	Ward & Administration
Yes	12	11	7
No	19	24	21

$x^2 = 1.2787$; ns; df = 2

This finding should also be juxtaposed against the Process data just reported. The Level of Staff factor had perhaps the least convincing apparent impact on decision-making processes, yet the dependent variable data here argue that simple structural variables may be equally, if not more, important for innovation decisions as changes in "perceived" participation.

Correlational Relationships Between Innovation Implementation and the Process-Attitudinal Dimensions

In order to explicate further the longitudinal relationships between Phase I process measures and innovation, several correlational analyses were performed. Seven scale scores from the three questionnaires (Workshop Decision Questionnaire, Workshop Effectiveness Questionnaire, and Consultation Decision Questionnaire) and a set of organizational process measures were the principal predictor variables in these analyses. (Since the unit of analysis for these correlations was the hospital, rather than the individual respondent, some data aggregation procedures were employed. As a function of that process, the two readiness scales were combined into a single overall Readiness for Change scale.)

Two types of dependent variables, or criterion variables, were employed in the correlations. One omnibus Innovation Decision score was computed by combining the yes-no workshop and consultation decisions into a one, two, or three score. In addition, Degree-of-Implementation scores, as described on page 70, were included in the analysis. These implementation Scores encompassed 90 to 360 days of follow-up after Phase I activities had terminated.

Scale scores and innovation

Several statistically, and conceptually, significant relationships were found between the change scores and the seven scales dimensions (see table 4.10). As was found in the Fairweather, Sanders, and Tornatzky study (1974), the Participation I and Participation II scores were both related to the Innovation Decision score.

Interestingly, the Social Influence scale, measured at the time of the consultation decision process, remained significantly related to all four Implementation scores taken over the year, though it was not significantly related to the Decision score. Although the magnitude of these implementation correlations decreased over time, the Social Influence scale was the only dimension that maintained a statistically significant relationship with change over all of the five measurement periods. This finding is of interest because Social Influence, though moder-

Table 4.10. Correlations Between Change Scores and Attitude–Decision Process Dimensions.

Scale	Innovation Decision Score	Degree of Implementation			
		90 days	180 days	270 days	360 days
1. Participation I	.4981***	.2814	.1508	.1413	.1157
2. Philisophical Congruity	.3225***	.0901	.1061	.0135	-.0922
3. Organizational Tenure	-.1562	-.3098*	-.0575	-.0712	-.0467
4. Program Distinctiveness	-.0981	.0902	-.2460	-.1375	-.1927
5. Overall Readiness for Change	.2845***	.1828	.0836	.0264	-.0676
6. Participation II	.2281*	.3255*	.2344	.2089	.1213
7. Social Influence	.1403	.5081***	.4104**	.3558*	.2941*

n = 31

n = 108

*p < .05
**p < .01
***p < .005

ately related to the early decision score, was highly correlated with activities more directly related implementation. These data suggest that there may be a discontinuity at organizational processes when one moves from verbal behavior - decision making and discussion in Phase I - to action - implementation in Phase II. To the extent that the Social Influence index is a crude proxy for delegation of authority, this finding highlights the importance of line staff involvement in actually carrying out implementation.

Staff's attitudes toward the Lodge innovation (Philosophical Congruity) and their perception of "Readiness" were only significantly related to the Innovation Decision score. These data did vindicate the utility of the "readiness" concept for adoption decision, but they did not support the specific, supposedly independent components of the AVICTORY formulation (Davis, 1973), nor their ability to predict implementation.

Subsidiary correlational analyses

In addition to the correlations with scale scores discussed above, further analyses were carried out with the archival and miscellaneous organizational process data mentioned above. The results obtained tended to reinforce the picture of innovation processes that we have been attempting to portray - of the importance of participation and delegation of authority.

Before looking at the details of this anlysis, there are several terms and variables that need redefining. As described in the Procedures section of chapter 3, during our interventions with the hospitals, one person at any one time functioned as our contact, or liaison to the project. Initially, this was always the superintendent, but more often the identity of the contact changed one or more times during our months of interaction. Thus, by gathering data on the status and role of the contact, considerable insight could be gained in emerging organizational processes.

A second important person has been briefly mentioned on page 85, the "sociometric star" whose existence was inferred from secondary analysis of the questionnaire. This was the person who was identified by peers on their questionnaires as being especially prominent in group decisions and discussions.

With regard to the contact and sociometric star, two descriptor variables are of particular importance. One was the administrative role of the person, which on a five-point scale measured the degree to which a person fulfilled a position high in the administrative hierarchy, versus being closer to the delivery of services per se. A second dimension was related to status attributable to professional discipline, with physicians being on the high end of this status dimension, and nurses being on the lower end.

First, let us examine the first, second and third rows on table 4.11 to consider how the disciplinary status of the sociometric star and/or contact relates to innovation adoption and implementation. As can be readily seen, having a lower level discipline for the sociometric star at the time of the workshop decision, and at the time of the consultation decision, was related to a high Innovation Decision score. The importance of involving lower level status staff early in discussion is most readily apparent in row 1. Here, having a lower status person (e.g., non-physician) as the center of discussion at the time of the workshop decision significantly correlated (r = -.52) with degree of implementation a year later.

One other variable related significantly to the Innovation Decision Score, but was of minor conceptual interest. A greater number of days taken to make the workshop decision correlated positively with the adoption decision (row 7). Of extreme interest, however, are the data concerning the role of the contact during our interaction with the hospitals (rows 4-6). Apparently having nonadministrative types as the contact at the time of the workshop is related to positive Innovation Decision scores, but not to subsequent Degree-of-Implementation scores. This is a fascinating reversal and demands additional comment. One can surmise that this reversal revolves around the different implications that the Innovation Decision and Degree-of-Implementation scores have for a hospital. The former is a series of verbal commitments; the latter represents tangible implementation behaviors. What these data suggest is that as an organization moves closer toward actual implementation, a more identified power-based, administrative sanction or presence is needed. During implementation, someone in a high administrative role has also to be involved.

Although fragmentary, these data can be construed as providing support for the notion of "product champion" or "bureaucratic entrepreneur" (Lambright, 1977). In effect, the data indicate that a person, or persons, needs to become an early advocate of the innovation, facilitate discussion about it, and over time, nudge the organization closer and closer to implementation. However, these data also extend and refine some of the concepts. Thus, while it appears that both participative discussion and decision making, and "bureaucratic entrepreneurship," are important as the organization moves from initial awareness of an innovation through implementation, the roles of the actors involved may change over the course of the process.

Table 4.11. Selected Correlations Between Archival Data and Innovation Implementation.

Scale	Innovation Decision Score	Degree of Implementation			
		90 days	180 days	270 days	360 days
1. Discipline Status of Sociometric Star for Workshop Decision	-.2032* (n=108)	-.4041**	-.4803***	-.3577*	-.3605*
2. Discipline Status of Consultation Decision Contact	-.2463** (n=91)	-.0031	-.0827	-.0635	-.0256
3. Lowering of Contact's Discipline Status --Initial Contact to Workshop Decision	.1582* (n=107)	.2965*	.3214*	.3299*	.2942*
4. Role of Contact at Workshop	-.2208* (n=107)	-.1054	-.0802	-.0974	-.1066
5. Role of Contact at Consultation Decision	-.2310* (n=94)	.2769	.3168*	.2812	.3774*
6. Change in Contact's Role - Workshop to Consultation Decision	-.0179 (n=80)	.3490*	.3793*	.3001*	.3265*
7. Number of Days to Workshop Decision	.2666** (n=108)	-.1271	-.3067*	-.3947**	-.3410*
8. Continuity of Staff from Initial Contact to Workshop Decision	.2259* (n=87)	.2053	.0552	-.0598	-.2217

n = 31

*p < .05
**p < .01
***p < .005

95

ORGANIZATIONAL CHARACTERISTICS AND
INNOVATION DECISIONS

The comparative and associational data thus far presented have been well within the mainstream of normal parametric and nonparametric analyses. Although these discussions have alternately considered the person or the hospital organization as the appropriate unit of analysis for the evaluation of experimental effects, little consideration has been given to the role of the organization per se in the reported results. In other words, independent of the experimental manipulations under scrutiny here, what is the the evidence for the importance of pre-existing organizational characteristics in the innovation process? In the two following sections, we present data relevant to this. Incidentally, these data begin to make the case for using organizational type as an explanatory and predictive concept.

The Evidence for Organizational Differences

In the preface to our presentation of the Analysis of Variance of questionnaire data (see page 75), it was pointed out that, for design and analysis purposes, the Hospital factor was nested within treatment cell (Winer, 1971). Thus, in analyzing the effects of the treatments on individual respondents' behavior, the effects of experimental treatment and unique organizational climate considerations could and should be separated.

Table 4.12 presents significance tests of this hospital factor for each of the eight questionnaire scales. As can be seen, there are extravagantly high levels of statistical significance attributable to the hospital factor. Metaphorically speaking, the hospital factor virtually swamps the effects of the experimental conditions, but what do these data mean in a conceptual sense?

Comparing the significance levels, or more intuitively, the absolute magnitude of differences, it appears that the reactions of an individual respondent in our sample could be more easily predicted on the basis of organizational affiliation than on the basis of treatment cell. One could say that the level of Participation, or Influence, or Readiness for Change, is at least as much a manifestation of the ongoing, relatively stable characteristics of the organization, as of ephemeral "change agent" encounters. In addition, it could mean that the particular response of an organization, and of individuals within the organization, to innovation-related technical assistance may be contingent upon the distinct characteristics of that organization. However, to say that different types of

Table 4.12. Hospital Significance.

Time	Instrument and Scale	Results		
		F	p	df
T_1	Workshop Decision Questionnaire			
	Participation I	1.694	›.002	72, 193
T_2	Workshop Effectiveness Questionnaire	F	p	df
	Philosophical Congruity	2.287	›.0005	72, 1497
	Organizational Tenure	2.569	‹.0005	72, 1497
	Program Distinctiveness	2.077	›.0005	72, 1497
	Organization Readiness for Change	3.892	›.0005	72, 1497
	Staff Readiness for Change	3.853	›.0005	72, 1497
T_3	Consultation Decision Questionnaire	F	p	df
	Participation II	2.852	›.0005	72, 779
	Social Influence	1.424	›.015	72, 779

97

organizations probably exist is merely stating the obvious;
whether meaningful typologies can be developed is another
question. A number of analyses, discussed below, were
addressed to this issue.

Empirically Typologizing Organizations:
Phase I data

In order to determine further the extent to which distinct
organizational characteristics influenced and moderated the
effect of our experimental manipulations, an attempt was made
to create an empirical typology of the Phase I sample of
hospital organizations (McKelvey, 1975). Multivariate techniques were employed, and the data base for developing the
typologies consisted of seven scale scores (see pages 53 to 56)
from the three questionnaires administered during the Phase I
experiment. The specific procedure employed was Tryon and
Bailey's (1970) O-analysis, or object analysis. .

Each of the hospitals was given a score on each of the
seven scales based on aggregation of individual response data.
These aggregate scores were then cluster analyzed, with the
unit of analysis being the organization. The results of that
data reduction yielded two dimensions, labeled Overall Participation and Innovation Attitudes respectively.

Each individual hospital was then assigned a score on
each of the two factors. Thus, for example, an individual
hospital X might be high on Overall Participation and low on
Innovation Attitudes. These data were then subjected to
O-analysis procedures.

In the object analysis procedure, objects (in this case
hospitals) are grouped in terms of homogeneous patterns of
score profiles. In effect, groups of objects (hospitals) are
assigned to sectors of multidimensional geometric space. Thus,
if a number of hospitals have a patterning of scores similar to
our example - hospital X above - then they would collectively
become a "type," or O-Type. Obviously, the number of
possible score sectors would increase geometrically with the
number of factors or dimensions involved.

Applying these procedures to the Phase I data base
yielded six O-types. Seventy-eight hospitals were assigned to
an O-type; 30 hospitals were discarded as idiosyncratic
singlets. Figure 4.5 depicts the patterning of factor scores
for each of the O-types, and the composition of the two
omnibus factors.

However, in order to argue the utility of the O-typing
procedure, it ought to have some explanatory or predictive
power. Two predictive - actually "postdictive" - exercises
were undertaken in connection with the above typologies. In
other words, what does membership in a group imply for

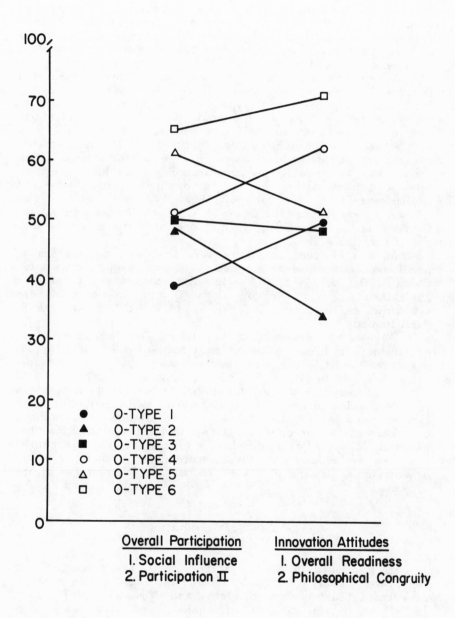

Fig. 4.5. Phase I O-types.

predicting innovation-related behaviors, rather than specific scores on a set of predictor variables?

Figure 4.6 depicts data on the percentage of members of each of the O-types that responded positively on the consultation decision. In other words, these are the percentages of hospitals that verbally committed themselves to an attempt to implement the innovation.

As can be seen there are wide disparities between the O-types. Seventy-five percent of O-type 6 were volunteers, while only 22 percent of O-type 1 made a verbal commitment to implementation. Clearly, different "types" or organizations responded differently to the interventions.

A second type of prediction involved the 31 hospitals that eventually became the sample for Phase II consultation activities. These were all organizations which had agreed to attempt implementation of the innovation. The Degree of Implementation scores for 90, 180, 270, and 360 days of follow-up are graphed in figure 4.7. Each of the original six O-types is represented if it had one or more hospitals that made it to Phase II.

As can be seen in figure 4.7, the O-typing has similar predictive power when applied to these longitudinal data. Clearly, O-types 5 and 6 are "high change" types of organizations. Reconsideration of the O-type profiles on figure 4.5 indicates that both O-types 5 and 6 are high on Overall Participation.

Obviously, this typologizing is only of a rudimentary, exploratory nature. A major drawback of the analysis just presented is with the data being used to form the organizational information. In this sense, we are not "predicting" at all. The respondents to the questionnaires were not drawn from a random sample of organizational personnel, but were instead persons who had talked to us, attended a workshop, or received a brochure. This obviously attenuates the generalizability of the findings. However, in subsequent chapters we will extend these procedures further by using organizational process data collected during other stages of the project.

The Ten Year Stability of
Organizational Characteristics

As was mentioned in the literature review, the researchers in the present study were also involved in a similar dissemination experiment (Fairweather, Sanders, and Tornatzky, 1974) circa 1967-71. In the context of that study, data were also gathered on organizational processes in general, and on decision-making variables in particular. Serendipitously, five questionnaire items administered to hospital staff in 1966-67

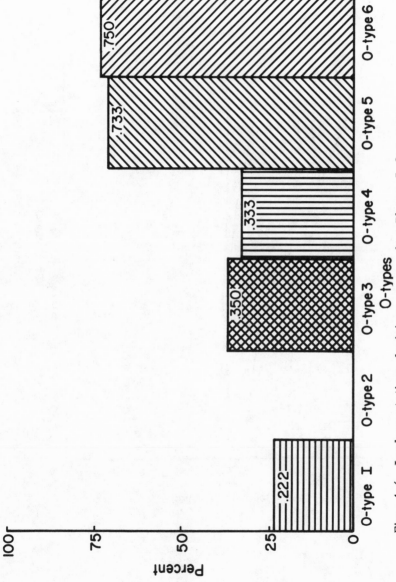

Fig. 4.6. Implementation decision scores by Phase I O-types.

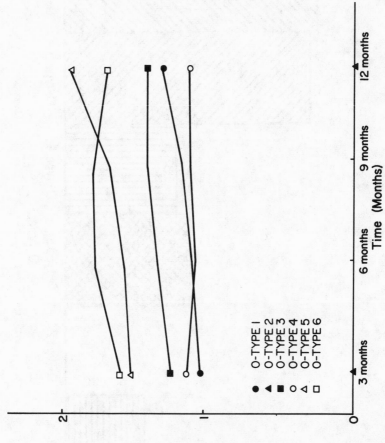

Fig. 4.7. Movement toward change by Phase I O-types.

exactly paralleled or duplicated items administered in 1976 during the current study. This permitted a pre-post examination of the longitudinal persistence of organizational processes over nearly a decade.

A group of 37 hospitals was identified that had data sets available for both time periods. Of the five questions, four dealt with decision making per se, such as the "amount of discussion," "personal involvement," and the like. A fifth item deal with felt satisfaction with the yes-no decision of whether to implement the Lodge innovation. In addition, the earlier data base had not only agregated responses, but also separated out the responses of the superintendent and the "contact person." Because of slightly dissimilar procedures used in the present study, the latter two data points were unavailable for the current data.

This suggested constructing a 5 x 15 correlation matrix for determining the relationship between the 1976 data (5 variables) and the 1967 data (15 variables).

Of the 75 Pearson product-moment correlations of most interest, the majority were both statistically insignificant and of minimal magnitude. Thirty-five of the 75 were below .10 in absolute value. Inspection of the matrix did yield some surprising relationships.

Of obvious interest is the relative persistence of the felt satisfaction with the decisions about the innovation. In contrast to the decision-making process variables, which generally showed a low level of long term association, several noteworthy correlations were obtained concerning satisfaction. For example, the mean rating across all staff of decision satisfaction correlated .26 between 1967 and 1976 ($p < .06$). More substantially, the aggregate felt satisfaction of 1976 correlated highly ($r = .40$; $p < .01$) with the 1967 contact person's perception of staff satisfaction with the decision. In addition, the 1967 amount of involvement by staff in the innovation decision (as perceived by the contact) correlated .50 with 1976 satisfaction ($p < .05$). All of this after a time span of nearly ten years.

Although it is difficult to develop firm conclusions from these data, some preliminary interpretations are possible. There does appear to be some long-term stability of organizational characterisitcs, but, based on these data, they do not appear to be organizational processes such as participative decision making. Rather, what may persist are organizational values and norms. Satisfaction with decisions persists and, it should be pointed out, the decisions made by the group of organizations were overwhelmingly not to implement the Lodge innovation. If staff felt satisfied with their decisions in 1967 and 1976, it may be because the rejection of the Lodge innovation was compatible with their organizational ethos, and the "right" decision for them.

Table 4.13. Correlation Matrix of Ten Year Stability
of Participative Decision Making.

1976 Data	Contact's Perception: 1967 Data				
	Extent of Staff Involvement in Decision Making	Personal Involvement	Discussion with Staff	Extent of Discussion with Other Staff	Satisfaction with Decision
Workshop Participants' Influence	.3212 (n=15)	.0842 (n=34)	.2135 (n=34)	.1766 (n=34)	.2054 (n=34)
Group Discussion by Decision Makers	.2260 (n=15)	.0499 (n=34)	.1469 (n=34)	.1528 (n=34)	.1485 (n=34)
Discussion by Staff at Large	.1859 (n=15)	.2057 (n=34)	.1131 (n=34)	.0601 (n=34)	.0357 (n=34)
Personal Involvement in Decision Making	.1139 (n=15)	.1366 (n=34)	.0893 (m=34)	.0310 (n=34)	.2481* (n=34)
Satisfaction with Decision Making	.5047** (n=15)	-.0958 (n=34)	.2409* (n=34)	.1939 (n=34)	.4033*** (n=34)
	Superintendent's Perception: 1967 Data				
Workshop Participants' Influence	.2555 (n=19)	.0129 (n=18)	.0301 (n=18)	-.0671 (n=19)	.1430 (n=19)
Group Discussion by Decision Makers	.0501 (n=19)	-.0954 (n=18)	-.2380 (n=18)	-.2990 (n=19)	-.0361 (n=19)
Discussion by Staff at Large	-.0579 (n=19)	.1533 (n=18)	-.2824 (n=18)	-.2848 (n=19)	.0078 (n=19)
Personal Involvement in Decision Making	.0713 (n=19)	.1217 (n=18)	-.1817 (n=18)	-.2800 (n=19)	.1605 (n=19)
Satisfaction with Decision Making	.2904 (n=19)	-.0320 (n=18)	.1916 (n=18)	.0309 (n=19)	.1739 (n=19)
	Grand Mean: 1967 Data				
Workshop Participants' Influence	-.0297 (n=37)	.0103 (n=37)	.0543 (n=37)	.0851 (n=37)	-.0523 (n=37)
Group Discussion by Decision Makers	.0113 (n=37)	-.0902 (n=37)	-.0759 (n=37)	-.0046 (n=37)	-.0805 (n=37)
Discussion by Staff at Large	.0148 (n=37)	-.0438 (n=37)	-.0423 (n=37)	-.0450 (n=37)	.1106 (n=37)
Personal Involvement in Decision Making	-.0114 (n=37)	.1844 (n=37)	.1504 (n=37)	.1626 (n=37)	-.2591* (n=37)
Satisfaction with Decision Making	.0884 (n=37)	.0352 (n=37)	.1775 (n=37)	.1322 (n=37)	-.2617* (n=37)

*p < .10   **p < .05   ***p < .01

Obviously, these data are fragmentary. It does appear that a promising line of future research needs to be pursued. If the norms and expectations of an organization do transcend turnover and the vicissitudes of time, this has important theoretical and policy implications.

SUMMARY AND CONCLUSIONS:
PHASE I EXPERIMENT

The principal findings of the Phase I experiment can be summarized as follows:

1. The participative decision-making processes of a public bureaucracy can be altered through the use of relatively simple and brief intervention techniques;
2. Participation enhancement techniques which focus on process (altering the intensity and frequency of inter-action) as opposed to structure (altering the number and organizational roles of decision participants) will produce a greater degree of perceived participation by organization members;
3. Participation enhancement techniques which focus on structure as opposed to process will be more likely to produce actual decisions for innovation;
4. Favorable attitudes toward an innovation, in the form of perceived Philosophical Congruity, and a sense of Overall Readiness to Change, seem related to decisions to implement, but only marginally to implementation per se;
5. Felt Participation seems again to be correlated with innovation implementation;
6. There is considerable evidence for the presence of pre-existing Organizational Characteristics which override the effects of brief participation enhancement techniques;
7. There is evidence for the longitudinal stability of Organizational Characteristics, and for the utility of attempting to construct organizational typologies.

As a precursor to the Phase II experimental results, two general conclusions can be drawn from the above summary list. First, a continued focus on organizational processes and decision making, as it relates to innovation, seems worthwhile, but it also appears that the intensity of intervention techniques must be considerably elevated in order to impact significantly on innovation implementation. In the next chapter, the encouraging results obtained from just such an approach will be described.

5 Organization Development and the Implementation of an Innovation

A major theme of previous chapters was that innovation processes are enhanced in organizations with less hierarchical and bureaucratic structures, and a more interactive style of decision making (Havelock and Havelock, 1973; Hage and Aiken, 1970). Our reasoning was that organizations that are not averse to the introduction of uncertainty - an inevitable byproduct of innovation - are more likely to have the capacity to cope with change. To the extent that an organization is bound by inflexible rules, formalistic modes of communication, and role specialization, a situation of amenability to innovation is not likely to prevail.

Nevertheless, a description of what might be a desirable state of affairs from the standpoint of innovation processes leaves the question of how to arrive at that state unanswered. This chapter describes the results of an experiment in employing Organizational Development techniques to that end.

ON CHANGING ORGANIZATIONAL SYSTEMS

There is considerable theoretical and tactical disagreement over the optimal way to introduce innovation into an organization. Change emanating from within the organization is one alternative but is not likely to be a high probability occurrence. This is not to deny the value, and enhanced credibility of peer-to-peer change agent activity (a topic that will receive considerable attention in the remaining chapters), but it should be acknowledged that there are organizational constraints that reduce the likelihood of innovation as a spontaneous occurrence. People within an organization have specific roles, bounded by certain rules and responsibilities.

Acting as an advocate for an innovation would upset or violate those constraints, and consequently the resistance to the role deviation would interfere with any efforts to alter the organization. Additionally, if the change advocate were a high echelon organizational member, change would also be unlikely because of the natural negativism to imposed innovation. It would be another example of decision making emanating from the top directed down to those in subordinate positions. One hospital staff member's spontaneous comments about this type of system are instructive:

> The administration decides and the line staff does the work, according to the rules set up by the hot shots. We have little or no say in any of the decisions. Sometimes they listen, but the decisions are already made, and we have no influence or input into them.

The drift of the discussion thus far is to argue for external assistance in the implementation of an innovation, but that external assistance ought to be formulated with an eye to the formidable nature of the implementation task. As described elsewhere (Hall and Loucks, 1977; Giacquinta, 1978), the implementation of innovations is at best an uncertain process and has, at worst, the potential for fiasco.

One type of external assistance is represented by the Organization Development movement. Organization development is often described as an effort directed towards bringing planned, organized change in order to "increase organizational competence" (Huse, 1975). Organization development is an attempt to improve the problem-solving and renewal processes of a group, particularly through a more effective and collaborative management of organizational culture (Huse, 1975). Implicit in the organization development change effort is the assumption that the role of a change agent is primarily to act as a catalyst, to increase the problem-solving capacity of an organization. The literature of Organization Development is explicitly not biased toward innovation per se. To quote one rather succinct statement of the Organization Development ideology:

> Change is not a primary task of the interventionist. To repeat, the interventionist's primary tasks are to generate valid information, to help the client system make informed and responsible choices, and to develop internal commitment to these choices. (Argyris, 1970)

Thus, while most OD consultants attempt to bring about increased openness and trust, and increased participation and sharing of power, they avoid the overt use and influence. In fact, most of the literature argues that the OD consultant should not assume the directive role of an expert and should not prescribe solutions to organizational clients, but should facilitate a meaningful search process for solutions (Ferguson, 1969; Schein, 1969; French and Bell, 1973). In many ways, such a stance is at odds with the problem of innovation implementation as we have defined it. If the goal of innovation-related technical assistance is to achieve reasonable replicates of proven material and social technologies, then a completely nondirective stance seems irrelevant.

Some Lessons from Diffusion Research

Diffusion studies (Fairweather, Sanders, and Tornatzky, 1974; Rogers and Shoemaker, 1971) have, to some degree, dealt with the problem of implementing an innovation in organizational systems. However, although much has been contributed in terms of the characteristics of adopters, and of crucial variables in the persuasion process, little is known about ways to optimize the interventions so as to impact significantly on organizational processes. It is clear that a certain amount of support, either from the top administration or from opinion leaders within an organization, is crucial to the furtherance of an innovation effort. It is also clear that support and commitment need to be nurtured among those charged with actual implementation. How to bring about these circumstances remains obscure.

One useful concept from the diffusion tradition is that of the adoption unit, defined by Rogers and Shoemaker (1971) as the "individual, group, or other unit that adopts the innovation" (p. 302). The functioning of the adoption unit is crucial for the longitudinal process of implementation, particularly with highly complex innovations that demand cooperation among members of an organization.

Innovation requires a support group both to sustain the staff's interest and to carry out the complex tasks necessary for full implementation. Not only must the adopting group, or unit, be open and reponsive to group planning and group decision making, it must be able to exist in an organizational climate that often provides little more than benign neglect. It would be unrealistic to expect an organization to welcome innovation unequivocally.

In the most relevant research related to the issue of innovation implementation in a hospital setting, Fairweather, Sanders, and Tornatzky (1974) empirically confirmed many of these notions. In that earlier research it was found that the presence of a viable adopting group in the hospital was necessary to spearhead the implementation effort; as they concluded:

It seems clear that a certain delegation of communication authority to lower status contacts is related to adoption. In the development of the adoption phase, we found that planning for group development was highly related to all other aspects of lodge adoption. Finally . . . we found effective and ineffective hospitals differed on the degree of "groupness" manifested in these meetings.

Thus, it appears that a small social change group within the organization that promotes the change effort is necessary to provide leadership in the change process.

...This is another indication that the adoption of social innovation is much more complex that the analogous process related to hula hoops and hybrid corn. Since an innovation such as the lodge is so highly complex it takes a group of people continually working for adoption if adoption is to occur. The data also indicate that the group must be a group, and not merely a collection of people. In other words, the adopting unit must be a cohesive group of interacting and committed people. (Pp. 190-191.)

The thrust of these findings, and other recent studies in innovation processes (Eveland, Rogers, and Klepper, 1977), is that attention needs to be focused on understanding, and impacting upon, organizational processes supporting implementers, particularly the group dynamics of the adopting unit. However, as bemoaned by Rogers (1975) some years ago, almost none of the existing innovation research has focused on stages and roles in the innovation process, in which the unit of analysis is the organization. The results described in this chapter will begin to bridge that gap.

Diffusion and Organization Development

The operative hypothesis of the Phase II experiment is that if there were a marriage of diffusion ideology and concepts with selected organization development techniques, interventions could simultaneously loosen bureaucratic structures and processes, and persuade and assist organizational members to implement innovation replicates fully. Organization Development, as usually practiced, is mainly a re-educative strategy designed to make staff more open and communicative. The focus is on work groups rather than on individuals within the organization. This makes it possible to emphasize group processes necessary for change, such as group decision making, group planning, and group problem solving (French and Bell, 1973). As noted earlier, longitudinal implementation of an innovation is more likely to occur if a small, cohesive, problem-oriented group is established within the organization, with a leader who will continuously push for change and keep the group moving toward its goal. An intervention like Organization Development would seem ideally suited to make an adopting group in an organization more open and more responsive to group planning and group decision making.

This type of organization development role is obviously more directive and action-oriented than the traditional view. Our review of innovation processes would suggest that the collaborative, nondirective format of the traditional organization development consultant might profitably be replaced with that of one who actively works with a group to help it implement a well-specified social innovation. This brings us to the hypothesis of the current research. The merging of organizational development techniques and the tradition of directive innovation diffusion that is advocated here, has heretofore not occurred. Rarely have these two traditions of practice and conceptualization been combined. Prior to this research, there has never been an experimental test of this possibility. What follows is the test.

EXPERIMENTAL DESIGN AND HYPOTHESES

The Phase I experiment examined various ways to facilitate participative decision making process instrumental to introducing innovation into an organization. Once a hospital was verbally committed to implementing the Lodge program, the Phase II experiment began. The experiment addressed the need for continuous attention to the existing organizational procedures and structures that obstruct the adoption of an innovation, particularly within the context of the implementing group.

Sample

Thirty-one hospitals from the Phase I experiment agreed to attempt implementation of the Lodge innovation. These hospitals were randomly assigned to one of two experimental conditions, representing different types of consultation assistance. At the same time, the hospital was assigned to one of the three consultants, who had also been consultants in the Phase I experiment. The hospitals within conditions were balanced so that the consultants had an approximately equal number of hospitals in both conditions. The same consultant

worked with the assigned hospital throughout the second
experiment.

Conditions

The two consultation conditions that comprised the experiment
were a Task Consultation condition and a Task Consultation
plus Organization Development condition. The organization
development package (see pages 59 to 70) was designed to help
the adopting group develop into a cohesive, supportive team
capable of implementing the Community Lodge program in toto.
The Organization Development exercises and feedback were
purposefully tied to program implementation tasks. Hospitals
in both conditions could receive as many as four two-day
consultations. In the Task Consultation plus Organization
Development condition, the consultant presented the OD
exercises during the last several hours of the second day of
consultation. The OD intervention did not "replace" any of
the Task Consultation activities. In the Task Consultation
condition, the activities were merely drawn out a bit, more
breaks were used, and the consultation day may have been
foreshortened a bit.

Measurement

The two instruments used for the second experiment were the
Post Consultation Questionnaire and the Telephone Follow-up
Questionnaire. The former questionnaire was designed to
measure changes in organizational processes and adoption
group dynamics. The questionnaire was reduced into four
conceptually distinct scales, as follows: Internal-External
Control, Group Affect, Group Process, and Support (see pages
70 to 71 for a more explicit description of these scales).
Across the 31 hospitals, the $\underline{N}$ of individual respondents was
244.
    Data on Degree of Implementation of the Lodge innovation
was gathered via a series of follow-up phone interviews,
conducted for one year subsequent to the initial consultation.
Using a checklist procedure, a single ordinal Degree of
Implementation score was assigned to each of the 31 hospitals,
at each follow-up period.

Hypotheses

The hypotheses being tested in the Phase II experiment were
straightforward:

1. As a result of the Organization Development activities, subjects in the experimental hospitals would show significant changes on the four process scales;
2. In particular, the Task Consultation plus Organization Development should show changes on the Group Process scale in the direction of greater evidence of group planning, group decision making, and interaction;
3. The Task Consultation plus Organization Development condition was predicted to result in more implementation of the Lodge innovation than the Task Consultation condition.

A review of the results obtained over this longitudinal experiment follows.

RESULTS - PROCESS AND IMPLEMENTATION

Comparative Analysis - Process Data

The four process scales were analyzed using analysis-of-variance. However, as described on pages 73-74, for purposes of considering data from individual respondents, the analysis had to be approached as a hospital-within-cell nest. Preliminary tests and appropriate pooling procedures, as described by Winer (1971), were followed.

Of the four scales, only on Group Process were significant differences (F = 9.076; df = 1, 194; p<.01) found between conditions (see table 5.1). Subjects in the OD group had elevated Group Process scores compared to subjects in the non-OD condition. The Organization Development procedures had the predicted effect of enhancing group interaction.

Table 5.1.   Between Condition Comparisons
for Process Data.

Scale	F	p	df
Internal-External Control	.032	ns	1,214
Group Affect	2.013	ns	1,214
Group Process	9.009	< .003	1,194
Support	2.268	ns	1,209

Comparative Analysis - Degree of Implementation Data

Since implementation of the Lodge was a collective effort of an adopting group in the organization, for obvious reasons, hospitals were used as the unit of analysis for the outcome data analysis.

Although there was no significant difference between the two conditions, there was a highly significant condition-by-time interaction ($F = 3.459$; df = 3, 78; $p < .02$)(see table 5.2).

Table 5.2. Degree of Implementation.

	90 days	180 days	270 days	360 days
Organization Development	1.34	1.48	1.70	1.78
No Organization Development	1.46	1.50	1.45	1.54

Source	MS	F	p	df
Condition	.227	.231	ns	1
Time	.343	4.774	< .004	3
C X T	.249	3.459	< .020	3
Hospital	.981			26
H within T	.072			78

Hospitals in the OD condition had greater change cores at 270 and 360 days. There was a also a significant Time effect ($F = 4.774$; df = 3, 78; $p < .004$). As can be seen from inspection of figure 5.1, change scores monotonically increased for all hospitals from 0.4 at 90 days to 0.65 at 360 days. The importance of this finding cannot be overemphasized. This is one of the very few experimentally confirmed demonstrations that OD can enhance the implementation of a specific social innovation. Given our previous discussions about the longitudinal complexity of implementation, the fact that the effect of OD is interactive with Time is quite understandable.

Subsequent analyses showed that there was neither a consultant, nor condition x consultant interaction, significant effect.

As expected, not all hospitals received four consultations, but the dropout rate was nearly equal for conditions (see figure 5.2). Consequently, there was no significant difference between conditions on the number of later consultations. What

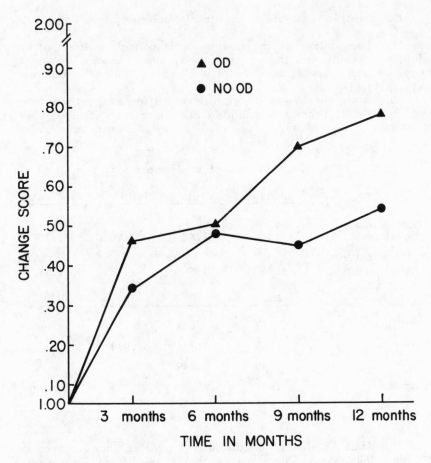

Fig. 5.1. Movement toward adoption by condition over time.

appeared to differ was what organizations did relative to implementation as a function of the two disparate types of consultation conditions.

Correlation of Process and Implementation Data

In order to articulate the relationship between organizational processes and implementation further, several correlational analyses were performed. The correlations depicted in table 5.3 indicate the relationship between the intervening processes of Support, Group Process, Affect, and Internal-External locus of control, and degree of implementation.

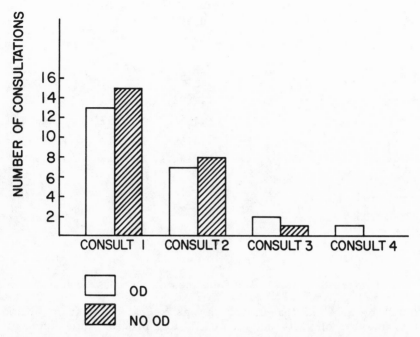

Fig. 5.2. Number of consultation visits for each condition.

        Not surprisingly, most of the scales do not correlate
significantly with implementation. However, Support and
Affect did correlate at acceptable levels of significance. It is
worth noting that the Support correlation decreases over time.
Although Support is unaffected by our experimental manipulations, it does appear that a minimum of external benign
neglect, and hopefully active support, is desirable for implementation to proceed. Likewise, the Affect correlation
indicates that some excitement at the beginning of implementation is indicative of change.

ORGANIZATIONAL CHARACTERISTICS AND
IMPLEMENTATION

In the previous chapter (pps 96-103), an empirical and conceptual case was made for the presence of enduring organizational characteristics mediating the course of innovation
processes in particular organizations, and moderating the
effect of external technical assistance and consultation. An
equivalent argument can be made, on the basis of the data,
for the Phase II experiment.

Table 5.3. Correlations Between Process Data
and Innovation Implementation.

Scale	90 days	180 days	270 days	360 days
Internal-External	.0630	.1892	.0455	.0110
Group Process	.0922	.1938	.2457	.2481
Affect	.3475*	.3759*	.1613	.1536
Support	.4758***	.5145***	.3863*	.3420*

n = 31

*p < .05
**p < .01
***p < .005

Omnipresent Hospital Differences on Process Scales

It will be recalled that Hospitals was a nested factor in all of
the analyses-of-variance computed for process questionnaire
data. As with the Phase I data, there were very large and
significant differences attributable to Hospitals in that analysis
(see table 5.4). The Hospital factor was significant for all the
scales except Group Process which, incidentally, was the only
scale showing a treatment main effect. Of particular salience
was the magnitude of the support scale finding. It appears
that the quality and quantity of central administrative support
of line staff is a distinguishing characteristic of hospital
organizations. Once again, the general conclusion to be drawn
from these data is the power and persuasiveness of something
akin to organizational climate influencing individuals' behavior.

Table 5.4. Between-Hospital Comparisons for Process Data.

Scale	F	p	df
Internal-External	2.06	< .002	28,214
Affect	1.795	< .011	28,214
Group Process	.937	ns	28,194
Support	4.351	< .0005	28,209

Empirical Organization Typologies

Once some salient characteristics of the hospitals in this study have been identified, it is again possible to use this information to differentiate the hospitals from one another to form typologies, or groupings of organizations. Once formed, the types can be differentiated and conceptualized in terms of distinctive profiles of organizational characteristics.

As in the previous chapter, O-analyses (Tryon and Bailey, 1970) were used to develop an empirical, multivariate typology. Using the four process scales, each hospital was given a score on each scale, which represented an aggregation of individual respondents' data. Using these data, hospitals were then grouped homogeneously into quadrants of geometric space, based on similarity of profiles of scores.

Six O-types were initially developed. Using hierarchical condensation procedures, two of these types were merged into other groups because of their limited membership. This yielded a final typology of four O-types, or object types. Their respective profiles on the four process scales are presented in figure 5.3.

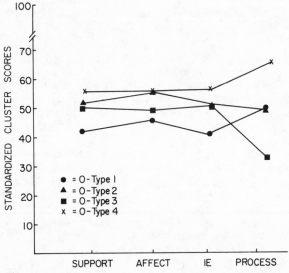

Fig. 5.3. PCQ Phase II O-types.

O-type 1 hospitals are medium on Process, and low on Support, Affect, and Internal-External Control. Hospitals in O-type 2 are medium on all the scales. O-type 3 comprises hospitals which are medium on Support, Affect, and Internal-External Control, and low on Process. O-type 4 hospitals are high on all the scales.

Once again, this typologizing on the basis of organizational characteristics had considerable predictive and discriminating power. If the mean implementation score over time is plotted for each O-type, the difference can be readily seen. O-type 4 hospitals moved the most toward full implementation, and O-type 3 hospitals moved the least toward implementation. Hospitals in O-types 1 and 2 are in between (see figure 5.4). If we look back at the O-type descriptions in figure 5.3, we can infer the effect of the scales on outcome. Process discriminates quite clearly between O-types. O-type 4 has the highest implementation score and the highest Process score; O-type 3 has the lowest implementation score and the lowest Process score. O-types 1 and 2 have medium implementation scores and medium Process scores. The Support, Affect, and Internal-External Control scales do not appear to discriminate between O-types as they relate to innovation processes.

DISCUSSION

Understanding and Utilizing the Effects of Organization Development

The results presented here represent a major advance in the organization development literature. This study is one of a very few to confirm experimentally the positive effect of organization development on group process and, more importantly, on organizational change. The organization development manipulations had an effect on both staff interaction and the hospitals as organizations. The Group Process scale results support our hypothesis on the effectiveness of OD in developing cohesive support groups and, by extension, the effect of such a group on implementation of an innovation.

The process results indicate that subjects in the Organization Development condition were much more "process-oriented" than subjects in the non-Organization Development condition, in that the manipulation was successful in fostering group planning and group decision making.

There was no difference between groups for the Support variable. Support did, however, correlate significantly with change, as did Process. It was noted earlier that the support correlation decreased with time as the Process correlation increased with time. We might speculate that both Organization Development and non-Organization Development groups sought out support from top management and discipline heads, but as time passed either the support or the need for it declined. Most likely the non-Organization Development group did not get anywhere in its efforts to move toward adoption,

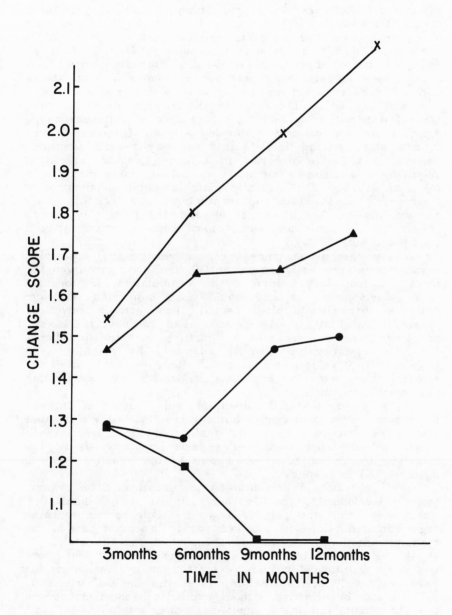

Fig. 5.4. Movement toward change by Phase II O-types.

and as their interest in adopting the program waned, so did their need for support. The Organization Development group, on the other hand, developed into a cohesive problem-oriented group, and their need for support likewise declined, but for a different reason.

The implementation results buttress this argument. While there was no difference between groups at 90 and 180 days (support and change correlations were highest; process and change were lowest), there was a significant difference at 270 and 360 days (support correlation was lowest; process correlation was highest). The delay in the OD group's implementation efforts can be looked at in a couple of different ways. First, it takes some time to develop a group (process) before it can start moving in a significant way toward adoption. Second, the Lodge program is a very complex innovation requiring role changes for staff as well as for patients. It takes an average of nearly six months to obtain administrative clearances and to start implementation. The lack of a difference between conditions at 90 and 180 days may simply reflect the lack of movement toward implementation in both conditions.

Given the circumstances (random assignment) by which organizations were assigned to the OD condition, and given the brief and transitory nature of the manipulation, few organization development experts would have supported our hypothesis that OD hospitals would show greater movement toward implementation. By no account did we have the luxury of either time or resources to nurture the kind of client/consultant relationship deemed advisable by much of the Organization Development literature. However, in light of the results, there are many important implications for organization development practice.

Many argue that OD consultants must be invited into an organization that is in crisis, but our results clearly show that this is not the case. In most instances, the hospitals with which we consulted were not experiencing a crisis at the initiation of our contacts. As shown by our results, crisis is not essential to change.

We were not invited into an organization to do organization development, but rather slipped the organization development past the gatekeepers. We made certain that the organization development was seen as an important part of the task consultation and, as such, important for the staff. It should be recalled that during the Phase I experiment there was some resentment voiced by staff when our manipulations were not clearly seen as helping them with the task at hand.

OD can be effective without explicit collaboration between the consultant and management personnel within the organization. The consultant did not rely on the clients' "felt need" for change and intervention as a guide for conducting the consultation. Because the OD intervention was tied to a specific innovation, the Lodge Program, the consultants focused on needs and problems whether or not staff identified them as such. Unlike usual OD consultants, we were very directive in our use of organizational advice. The results indicated that our OD style was effective and in many cases beneficial to the organization. Staff felt less stifled by organizational blocks and their morale improved as a result of being able to implement the Lodge program.

Finally, OD consultants have been either resistant to, or negligent about rigorous evaluation of organization development techniques. One expects that some of this is due to anxiety over negative results. Some consultants may feel that evaluation cannot capture the qualitative differences and changes that may occur as a result of organization development. This study suggests that even a simple, short-term intervention can produce positive results showing the effectiveness of organization development training.

When OD outcome studies are performed, they are frequently plagued with methodological problems. Frequently, OD interventions are variable and cover a number of organizational systems; in many cases, experimenters then find it difficult to standardize and compare the OD activities. One wonders if this is another result of the practitioner's fear of negative results. If one tries to hedge one's bets to ensure that OD is effective, the result is usually a muddled and confounded methodological mess.

Organizations and Change

Public service bureaucracies have not historically been the model of the "changeable organization." Psychiatric hospitals in particular represent a conservative and heavily bureaucratized public agency. This study, however, has demonstrated ways to effect meaningful innovation in a public service bureaucracy. A small change group within the organization can promote an innovation and overcome some of the natural bureaucratic resistances.

This research has also reflected the omnipresent organizational differences that pervade the mental health system and, by implication, most public service bureaucracies. The results showed that the organizational variables, like Affect and Interal-External Locus of Control, differ widely between hospitals, and are a function of organizational idiosyncrasies. Perhaps change agents should focus less on these finds of organization variables and more on group process kinds of variables.

Finally, it appears that organization developement is an effective way to increase the organizational viability of an

adopting group; OD also enhanced the implementation of the
Lodge program. OD can be used to develop a social change
group which can sustain staff's interest and carry out the
complex tasks necessary for implementing an innovation. The
results reported here have significance not only for change
agents as a means of increasing the likelihood of innovation
adoption, but also for OD consultants as an encouragement for
further research on the effectiveness of organization development.

A Summarizing Analysis and A Scenario

The thrust of the data presented in this and the previous
chapter is to reinforce our notions on the importance of
organizational process variables in innovation adoption and
implementation. Based on both experimental and correlational
data, the relationship seems too strong to deny.

What, cumulatively and phenomenologically, do these data
from Phase I and Phase II convey? As a way of capsulizing
the experimental and correlational data, we have constructed
two composite scenarios of successful and unsuccessful interventions. Both are extracted from "real" case history
materials.

The superintendent at Nervous State Hospital was contacted and told about the information and consultation assistance available to develop a Community Lodge program. The
decision makers for the workshop decision were physicians and
psychiatrists. Dr. Topman, a psychiatrist, was considered by
the decision makers the most involved person in the workship
decision. After many weeks, Dr. Topman decided that the
staff and the hospital were not likely to benefit from information and consultation assistance from the project staff and
declined the workshop offer.

A similar situation occurred at Uptight State Hospital,
but the main workshop decision maker, Dr. Incharge, decided the staff might derive some benefit from a workshop.
Dr. Incharge arranged the details for the workshop and
ordered staff to attend. Staff who attended the workshop
were interested but not enthusiastic.

A few weeks after the workshop, Dr. Incharge informed
us that he wanted the hospital to start a Community Lodge
program. He assigned the task of implementing the program to
one of the adult psychiatric discharge wards. Our new
contact become Dr. Yesman, also a psychiatrist, and an
underling of Dr. Incharge.

At the first consultation, staff had many excuses for not
being able to attend the consultation, which lasted two days.
In addition, the ward team leader had not been transferred
from her old ward to her new assignment and, consequently,

could not attend the consultation at all. Dr. Yesman was clearly going through the motions of trying to set up the small group ward, but he was doing so only because of Dr. Incharge's orders.

Over the next few months, more problems kept cropping up with no solutions in sight. After four months of almost no movement toward implementation, Dr. Incharge called to inform us that Uptight State Hospital was unable to set up the Lodge program due to insurmountable blocks made by the staff, the administration, and the state legislature.

A very different sequence of events took place at Serene State Hospital. After the project staff contacted the superintendent, he immediately referred us to Mr. Contented of the Social Work Department. Mr. Contented was perceived by the workshop decision makers as the person most involved in the workshop decision. A few days after our conversation, Mr. Contented informed us that he thought a workshop would be of great benefit to hospital staff, and granted us entry permission. After the workshop, Mr. Contented informed us that the staff were pleased with the workshop presentation and eager to utilize our consultation assistance. Mrs. Linestaff, a mental health worker and team leader, became our contact.

At the initial consultation, the staff were very excited about the prospect of starting a Community Lodge. A new staff was assembled for the purpose of starting a Lodge program. A building had been recently renovated and furnished specifically for the Lodge program. The first two-day consultation was scheduled so that it became part of a week-long hospital training program to implement the Lodge program. The Organization Development exercises unexpectedly dovetailed very well with the training the hospital provided.

The group picture exercise became especially relevant as it attacked a problem that had been plaguing the group all week, i.e., being told what to do. During the group picture exercise, the group, feeling very cooperative and noncompetitive, decided they didn't want to pick the best picture. The consultant insisted that they must. When he rejected their solution, which was to tape all the pictures together to form one large picture, they became angry. The group transferred their negative feelings toward the hospital administration to the consultant. It appeared that the group felt that the superintendent and chief of staff were always telling them what to do and not considering their needs and their input. After the consultant and the coordinator of the hospital training session pointed this out to the group, they were able to discuss the problem and eventually move on, without letting their negative feelings for the "front office" keep them from implementing the program. The hospital administration did support the program and staff's efforts to utilize it.

Six months later, staff were still excited, and still believed they were being supported. After almost a year, the excitement was more subdued, as they were making the final preparations for discharging their patients into a Lodge. However, they still felt supported, although not as much as they felt at the first consultation. This probably reflected their faith in their own abilities and in the effectiveness of the program, and resulted in a lessening of the need for support for their efforts.

Eleven months after the first consultation, the first Lodge was begun in downtown Serene. Staff and patients were hopeful and saw that their work had culminated in a well prepared and enthusiastic group of Lodge members.

Summary and Conclusions:
Phase II Experiment

The principal findings of the Phase II experiment can be summarized as follows:

1. The cohesiveness, interpersonal interaction, and dynamics of an adopting group can be altered via the use of organization development techniques as an adjunct to directive, task-oriented consultation;
2. The implementation of a social innovation can be enhanced by the use of organization development techniques as an adjunct to directive, task-oriented consultation assistance;
3. Organization development can be used in the context of a directive technical assistance/dissemination structure;
4. Administrative Support for change and the Group Process of the adopting group were significantly correlated with implementation;
5. As in Phase I, there is considerable evidence for the presence of pre-existing organizational characteristics, which to some extent override the effects of organization development intervention techniques; and
6. There is evidence for the utility of attempting to construct organizational typologies.

Taken together, the results of the Phase I and Phase II studies are convincing evidence for the usefulness of experimenting with alternative technical assistance, or "change agent," tactics. The externally-applied manipulation can impact on organizational innovation processes. In the next several chapters, we shift our perspective "inward" toward a closer examination of those processes as they occur in peer-to-peer professional interactions.

III

Studies in
Peer Processes

6 Indigenous Interaction and Innovation *

INTRODUCTION

At least two premises have guided the research activities described in the previous three chapters. One explicit assumption has been that the process of innovating is likely to produce uncertainty in organizations, and that the enhancement of participative decision making and group interaction can be used instrumentally to assist the innovation process. The Phase I and Phase II experiments were thus designed to compare various ways to impact on organizational processes and structures to this end.

A second implicit assumption, however, is embodied in the strategy of the Phase I and Phase II experiments. Both of these efforts emphasized the role of the <u>external</u> change agent, or consultant, in the innovation process, and in this sense they were well within the normative practice of the dissemination-of-innovation tradition.

Such an approach may not be entirely tied to the current realities of public sector innovation on a number of counts. In the case of public service bureaucracies, such as the sample in this research, there has historically <u>not existed</u> an explicit, well-structured, centrally-directed technical assistance network such as the one fielded in the Phase I and Phase II experiments. There is no clear analog to the agricultural extension system in the public service sector. (One exception to this has been the piloting of the National Diffusion Network, being developed by the U.S. Office of Education. After screening

---

*This chapter was written by Mitchell Fleischer, in collaboration with Esther Fergus.

educational innovations via the OD-NIE Joint Dissemination
Review Panel, new programs are disseminated to the field via
an elaborate training, consultation, and technical assistance
network, with a heavy involvement by the developers of the
innovations. This is quite an exciting and revolutionary
development in the public sector, and the reader is advised to
consult Emrick [1977] for a more complete description.) There
is no legitimate, highly visible, and national system to provide
public service bureaucracies with information and assistance
relating to social innovations. Some would argue that the
ERIC program in education is such a system. However, there
is little "hands-on," face-to-face consultation assistance (see
Fairweather, Sanders, and Tornatzky, 1974, for evidence on
the necessity thereof), and the system is oriented more toward
research findings than toward operationalized social innovations
and programs. Moreover, questions can be raised as to the
visibility and accessibility to practitioners of a system that
relies heavily on computerized information storage.

   This does not mean that "innovation" does not occur in
public service bureaucracies. It does, but it often does not
follow a dissemination/technical assistance mode. Much innovation in public agencies is locally inspired and guided. As
Berman and McLaughlin (1978) concluded from their study of
educational innovating, local talent and expertise are usually
used to formulate new programs. Aylen, et al. (1977) found
similar results indicating the importance of professional peers,
and local planning, in the innovation process.

   There are a number of explanations for this state of
affairs. One reason is that the effectiveness of social technology, as opposed to material technology, is rarely unambiguous. The incremental benefit of an "innovation" over
existing practice is often moot. Not surprisingly, testimonials,
and dubious self-reports (Scheirer, 1978), become equivalent
to evidence, and what a social innovation actually "is", is
unclear (Behr, 1978).

   Associated with the above is perhaps a heavier reliance in
the public service sector on innovation mediated by peer-to-
peer interaction. The potency of peer influence in the
diffusion of innovation, of course, has been widely documented
in the past. The classical studies of the diffusion of hybrid
seed corn among farmers (Ryan and Gross, 1943), and of
antibiotic drugs among physicians (Coleman, Katz, and Menzel,
1957), are well-known examples. In both studies, although
the salesperson or the detail person played an important role
in initially establishing the innovation in the market, informal
communication sources made the product more legitimate to
adopters.

   Given our previous comments about the uncertainty-
arousing effect of change, it should not be surprising that
peer-to-peer interaction could be facilitative of innovation.

Several years ago, Festinger (1954) described how people tend to use interaction as a social comparison process in situations of stimulus ambiguity, as a way of defining for themselves what social reality is. To the extent that participants in that interaction are more credible (Hovland and Weiss, 1951; Hovland, Janis, and Kelley, 1953), such interpersonal persuasiveness is likely to be enhanced.

Not surprisingly, there is also evidence to support the notion of peer influence as particularly credible in nature. Brock (1965) and Berscheid (1966) both provide data that relate credibility to shared attributes, or similarities, between parties to an interaction. Finally, to return to the innovation literature, Rogers and Shoemaker (1971) strongly argue that homophyly (similarity) between change agent and adopter will enhance innovation adoption.

To summarize, the literature suggests two simple conclusions: (1) the observational and empirical evidence suggest that indigenous, peer-to-peer interaction is an important component of innovation; and (2) indigenous, peer-to-peer innovation communication processes exist for good reasons of credibility, trust, and uncertainty reduction. In a parallel fashion, given that peer-to-peer communication about, and assistance with, innovation do exist, there are two general policy questions that need to be addressed, specific to the problem of innovation in the public sector:

1. What is the extent of spontaneously occurring indigenous exchanges of information? What is the nature of the infrastructure of innovation, and what are its incentives and disincentives, advantages and disadvantages? These general issues will be addressed in the remainder of this chapter and the next.
2. What externally-applied interventions can by employed to promote and facilitate the process of peer-to-peer diffusion of innovation? This issue will be addreseed in chapters 7,8,9 and 10.

DOES A NETWORK OF INDIGENOUS DISSEMINATION EXIST? AN EXPLORATORY STUDY

A Network Analysis of Innovation Interchange

As an initial incursion into the policy questions posed above, an attempt was made in the context of the present research to determine the extent of communication about new programs and innovation among our sample of hospitals. In effect, we were trying to discover the "base rate" of spontaneous exchange of information about innovations between members of different organizations - in this case, mental hospitals. In addition, although all communication of innovation involves individuals, it would seem useful to depict the nature of organizational networks that those person-to-person interactions encompass. This was a second objective of this exploratory research.

Rogers and Agarwala-Rogers (1976) have made a strong case for the consideration of networks in studying the innovation process. Communication networks discovered empirically often markedly deviate from the official organizational charts that ostensibly delineate them. Moreover, in determining the nature and extent of innovation communication, there is a need to extend the analysis from the intraorganizational to the interorganizational. From a policy perspective, it would be useful to know the answers to the following questions: How much exchange of new program information transcends state boundaries or regional groupings? What is the extent to which a definite network structure of such interchange occurs? What are the implications for interorganizational networks, such as they exist, for the problem of encouraging the implementation of replicates of proven innovations?

Fortunately, recent advances in analytic tools have made answers to these and similar questions more readily attainable. Computer technologies are available for capturing intraorganizational and interorganizational sociometries, a task which heretofore would have been intolerably laborious.

Method

The analysis

The specific analytic technique used in this study depicts networks of communication between individuals or organizations. The primary unit of analysis is the link between units (either individuals or organizations). The task of Network Analysis is to determine the structure of the network, based on the links. Elements of this structure can include groups of network members, who communicate more with each other than with non-group members, liaisons, who act as a communication path between two or more groups, and isolates, who have little or no outside communication.

William Richards' (1975) NEGOPY computer program takes raw data in the form of unit-to-unit links and can determine the structure of the network according to certain user-determined criteria. One feature of the Richards program is that it enables the user to weight each link according to some measure of importance. Thus, a link that was utilized frequently might be assigned a weight of "2," while a link used less frequently might receive a weight of "1." While these weights or "link strengths" are utilized internally by the program, they can also be used as minimum or maximum cutoff values. For example, if a user found he was not interested in links that had less than a certain strength, he could direct the program to ignore such links. Perhaps more importantly, this analytic tool enables the user to graph the sociometric structure of an empirically determined communication network.

The sample and the data

Data was collected from all 80 hospitals that received workshops. Since the primary focus in this study was on hospitals in the sample, links were considered for use in the network analysis if they involved communication between hospitals in: (1) the main sample of 108; (2) the sample of 24 from the Site Visit experiment (see chapter 9); (3) hospitals that were known as Lodge adopters (see page 110); and (4) one hospital that was widely known for its innovativeness in the deinstitutionalization of chronic mental patients. Thus, the "map" produced by this analysis could include as many as 142 state and federal mental hospitals.

Measurement

In order to determine the presence of innovation-related communication hospitals, respondents to the Workshop Effectiveness Questionnaire (see pps. 54-55) were asked to provide information about which hospitals and other institutions they had communicated with about new programs during the past year. Space was provided for the respondents to write in the names of these institutions and the number of individuals contacted at each. The exact format of the question can be seen in table 6.1.

Some notes on the data and their relationship with the NEGOPY program

Since the data were in the form of one-way links between hospitals, they included information about the communication behavior of hospitals from which data were not collected. In other words, if someone from hospital A claimed to have communication with someone from hospital B, then we have information about the A-B link, even though we have not asked hospital B about this. While it would certainly be desirable to confirm the presence of the link with hospital B, in the context of this study, such confirmation often could not be obtained. Even within the sample of hospitals from which data were collected, confirmation was not always available. This was because questionnaires were not completed by the entire hospital staff, but only be those staff who attended the

Table 6.1.   Network Question.

44. The next few questions attempt to determine how much
     contact you have with individuals from other mental
     hospitals or treatment facilities in the United States.
     Please list the names of the mental hospitals or treatment
     facilities with which you have had contact about new
     programs in the past year. In addition, please indicate
     the number of individuals you have had contact with at
     each organization.

Name of Hospital or Treatment Facility   Number of individuals
                                            contacted in past year

Name of Hospital or Treatment Facility	Number of individuals contacted in past year

workshop. Since only a small percentage of the staff of any
one hospital was questioned, the notion of attempting to obtain
confirmation of all the links seemed inappropriate.

     We acknowledge that the data presented here are an
incomplete representation of interhospital communication in the
United States. Data were collected from only 80 hospitals (of
142 included in the analysis and 250+ in the nation), and even
the data from those hospitals were incomplete since only
workshop participants provided answers to our questions.
While there are certainly "holes" in the data, there would still
seem to be every reason to believe that it is fairly repre-
sentative. The 80 hosptials that provided data might well be
considered more innovative than those that refused to have a
workshop, and thus might be considered as presenting a
"liberal" picture of the amount of innovation-related communication. The same can be said for the individual workshop
participants. Thus, our sample consists of a group of
hospitals and individuals who are perhaps more innovative and

consequently more communicative than average. Therefore, while the structure of the network described is no doubt incomplete, it seems to be a fairly good representation of what the complete network is like.

Two issues were immediately encountered when the analysis was begun. This was the problem of how to take data in the form of individual to hospital links (as obtained from the Workshop Effectiveness Questionnaire) and convert them into hospital to hospital links. Another problem was the assignment of weights (link strengths) to these links.

The first problem was solved by defining a hospital-hospital link as existing whenever an individual from one hospital claimed to have communicated with any other individual at another hospital. The weighting problem was more difficult. The initial intention had been to use the "number of individuals contacted" question (see table 6.1) as the basis for these weights. Unfortunately, few of the respondents to the questionnaire who indicated communication with other institutions answered this question. While it may be inferred that the respondents meant this to indicate only one contact, such an inference is questionable; thus, that question was not usable. A more workable alternative was then developed which involved using the percentage of all respondents from each hospital who indicated the presence of a link as the basis for the link strength; if there were 50 respondents to the Workshop Effectiveness Questionnaire from a hospital, five of whom indicated the presence of a particular link, the link received a weight of 10 (5/50 x 100). It should be noted that this weighting has the major advantage of being independent of the number of respondents to the questionnaire. A cutoff of 5 percent was established as the minimal percentage for the existence of a link. This figure was arrived at empirically as it yielded the clearest network structure in subsequent runs.

Results

The analysis performed by the NEGOPY program provides a variety of information. The primary output is in the form of a description of the structure of the network including group membership, descriptions of the roles of non-group members, and a description of all links betwen individual units and groups. This structure, as described by the program, can be transferred to a "map" so that the structure can be visually observed. An abbreviated version of this map can be seen in figure 6.1. The figure shows only those hospitals that were members of groups or were identified as liaisons. Although the entire map is too detailed to be displayed, the basic structure of the network is clearly shown. Of the 142 hospitals that could potentially be covered by this analysis, only

50 were identified as unambiguous members of the nine groups formed. Eight additional hospitals were identified as liaisons between these groups. Of the remaining 84 hospitals, 48 were identified as isolates (hospitals having one or no link with another hospital), and 36 so lacked a pattern that they could not be categorized and were therefore classified as "others."

From a policy perspective, these initial findings have interesting implications. When only 40 percent of a group of hospitals can be clearly identified as part of a network of innovation-related interorganizational communication, and furthermore, when an additional 35 percent can be designated as isolates from the mainstream of innovation, we cannot readily assume that improvements in mental health practice will be disseminated at anything other than a snail's pace.

The second striking feature of figure 6.1 is that the groups that exist seem to be determined almost exclusively by geographic proximity. People talk to people to whom they are close in distance. Thus, it can be said that, with a few exceptions, interhospital communication about innovation takes place primarily within a region or state. The obvious "provincialism" of the mental health innovation network has important policy implications.

The only major exception to this pattern was found among the Veterans Administration hospitals, which form a network of innovation communication among themselves. Unfortunately, while they are not geographically provincial like the state mental hospitals, the VA hospitals are organizationally provincial, staying within the boundaries of the federal system. It will be noted that there is virtually no communication between VA hospitals and state hospitals. Taken as a whole, the findings depicted in figure 6.2 yield a simple conclusion: a national network of interorganizational interaction about social technology (at least in the area of mental health) simply does not exist.

Further confirmation of these findings resulted from an additional analysis. This involved looking at all links between hospitals to find out which ones transcended regions (strictly defined as a hospital's state or a contiguous state) or organizational constraints (defined as the state or VA system). Of the 142 hospitals, 122 were found to have at least one interhospital link. Of these, 51 had at least one link that was both interregional and interorganizational. This is 42 percent of the communicating hospitals (36 percent of all 142 hospitals). However, of 384 total links in the study, only 79 (21 percent) were both interorganizational and interregional. A closer look reveals that seven hospitals were involved in 55 of these links. This means that "national" communication about innovation is really confined to only a very few hospitals. Although these organizations could be potential "linking pins" in a national network, this is not the case at present.

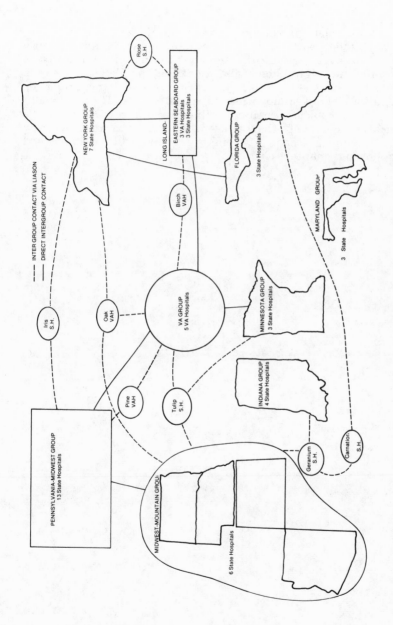

Fig. 6.1. Network analysis of psychiatric hospitals.

SUMMARY

Clearly no national innovation network exists at present among
mental hospitals, with which a change agent could usefully
connect. However, given the seven "linking pins" mentioned
above, and the eight hospitals identified as liaisons by the
analysis, it does seem that interorganizational peer-to-peer
communication about innovation is possible, and occasionally
occurs. The problem remains to find ways for enhancing the
communication channels that presently exist and to open new
channels. Several means of doing just that will be discussed
in the following chapters.

7 Promoting Innovation Communication Through Print Media: An Experiment

INTRODUCTION

Given the nonexistence of a national network of innovation-related communication as described in the previous chapter, a decision was made to try to promote one by fostering inter-hospital communication through a mass distribution of written materials. Several factors argue for the use of this method. From a practical perspective, written material is relatively inexpensive and can reach a large population without much staff effort. There is also some empirical evidence that suggests that written material might influence innovation adoption. For example, receiving written material seemed to have had some effect on mothers' consenting to polio vaccination for their children (Clausen, Seidenfeld, and Deasy, 1954). Another study, related to the adoption of family planning practices (Palmore, 1967), revealed that written information stimulated communcation and led to adoption.

Of course, there is considerable literature to indicate that written materials are not terribly effective in producing innovation adoption and implementation. A study of the effect of an ecology newsletter on environmental practices found that the exclusive use of newsletters were of no value in producing behavioral change (Lounsbury, 1976). Most directly relevant are two findings from the Fairweather, Sanders, and Tornatzky (1974) innovation dissemination study. There it was found that written brochures distributed to hospital staff were quite ineffective in producing a decision to adopt. In a subsequent phase of that sudy, it was found that the use of a written manual, as opposed to a face-to-face consultation, was less effective in facilitating implementation.

137

It should be pointed out, however, that media has rarely been examined as a means of enhancing communication between professional peers, between "innovators" and those who might be interested in innovation. In addition, certain historical events contemporary with this study supported the use of written material as a first step in promoting network growth. In 1978, the President's Commission on Mental Health devoted a great deal of attention to the issue of the chronic mentally ill, a population that can benefit directly from the Lodge innovation and similar programs. Seeking innovative solutions to the problems of this patient population appeared to be a new national priority. The creation of the Community Support Program within the National Institute of Mental Health (Turner and Tenhoor, 1978) at about this time seemed to add to the legitimacy of the Lodge as a noteworthy example of social technology.

The apparent shift in mental health policy relevant to the Lodge innovation, the national climate for adoption, the relative low cost of a newsletter, and the opportunity to reach large numbers of mental health professionals, became the factors supporting the creation of Lodge Notes, and a subsequent ten-month study of its impact on building communication between mental health personnel. Through the newsletter, we hoped to increase peer-to-peer communication among hospitals that had already implemented the Lodge innovation and, more importantly, between these "innovators" and other possible adopters. Throughout this newsletter study, the research staff adopted a relatively passive stance. The intention was to facilitate contact and communication between service providers, not to use the newsletter as an entree for more consultation by the research project staff. The ultimate goal was to help create something akin to a network of communication about the Lodge innovation.

EXPERIMENTAL DESIGN

A sample of 50 hospitals that had already received workshops on the Lodge innovation (see page 43) but had subsequently decided against adopting the innovation comprised the sample for the study. They were randomly assigned to one of two cells of an experimental design. The Experimental-Newsletter condition received the newsletter, Lodge Notes, for ten months; the Control condition did not receive the newsletter (see figure 7.1). Although there was some possibility that the Control condition may have been "contaminated" by staff receiving the newsletter through informal channels, it seems unlikely. Given the data described in the previous chapter concerning the weakness of national networking the possibility is low.

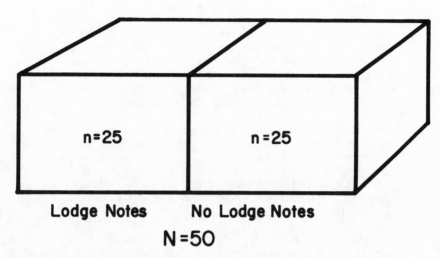

Fig. 7.1.   Lodge notes experimental design.

The mailing list for the newsletter was developed from the lists of participants from the initial workshop. In order to respect the wishes of the recipients, the readers had the option of refusing the newsletter by completing and mailing back a short form provided on the back page of each issue of the newsletter. Recipients could also request back issues and suggest new names to be added to the mailing list, thereby participating in network building. The newsletter mailing list for the experiment reached 600. (The total mailing list actually approached 3000 at the end of the overall study and included many people who were not involved in the experiment described in this chapter.)

The Newsletter

In keeping with a fine journalistic tradition, the newsletter was a two-page foldout, on cream-colored paper, with a black and green group silhouette as a logo, and the title Lodge Notes. As indicated above, the central theme of all the newsletter issues was to promote interaction between previous Lodge adopters and the curious. For example, in the first issue, the point was made that the newsletter was to be an innovators' newsletter and that participation was welcomed. Several methods were used to enhance the readers' perception that there was a role for them in the newsletter. The following excerpt is illustrative:

TO THE READERS: What You Can Do

Each month we will share letters which are directly
concerned with Lodge programs through the newsletter. We would like your help in answering
questions raised by our readers. Feel free to state
your reactions or offer alternative solutions to the
problems that other Lodge innovators are facing.

Let us know what's happening in your area. If you
have a project that you think is interesting, send us
information about it.

Send us a list of names complete with correct addresses of interested people who wish to be on the
newsletter mailing list. (Lodge Notes, June 1977)

More specifically, we asked the readers to state their interest
and ideas about the creation of a national network of Lodge
innovators:

CREATING A NETWORK OF LODGE ADOPTERS

The MSU-NIMH Innovation Diffusion Project wants to
create a communication network among people who
have adopted the Lodge program. Staff have been
thinking of several ideas for helping adopters become
involved with one another, and in furthering the
spread of the Lodge idea. Being considered are
activities such as involvement of adopters in workshop presentations at other hospitals, organizing
presentations at national conventions, and having
regular conference phone calls with the Innovation
Diffusion Staff. Newsletter articles will keep readers
posted as plans and activities directed toward
creating the network of adopters become clearly
defined. Do you have any additional ideas? (Lodge
Notes, June 1977)

To project the innovators' vital role further in the sharing of
news, a "Lodge Innovators" list was printed. One name from
each of the existing Lodge programs was listed, with the
address and institutional affiliation supplied. This section was
printed in each issue, with new adopters' names being added
as they implemented the program. Although the first issue
contained the names of nine program representatives, the list
expanded to 15 names by the last issue of the experiment.
A brief history of the Lodge innovation was printed in
the first issue to provide the adopters with some sense of
being a significant part of the dissemination process. The
highlights included completion dates of each of the programs:

A HISTORICAL PERSPECTIVE OF THE COMMUNITY LODGE

December 1963	-	First Lodge created at Palo Alto, California
March 1964	-	Lodge established at Topeka, Kansas
June 1966	-	Lodge established at Hot Springs, Arkansas
July 1967	-	Lodge established at Denver, Colorado
September 1967	-	National Diffusion of the Lodge Program funded by NIMH
September 1969	-	Community Life for the Mentally Ill (book on the Lodge) published
July 1970	-	Lodge established at Anchorage, Alaska
October 1970	-	Lodge established at Cleveland, Ohio
October 1974	-	Creating Change in Mental Health Organizations (book on Lodge diffusion) published
May 1975	-	MSU-NIMH Innovation Diffusion Project funded by NIMH
December 1976	-	Lodge established at Appleton, Wisconsin
April 1977	-	Lodge established at Knoxville, Tennessee
June 1977	-	First issue of Lodge Notes published.

A recurrent and popular fixture in Lodge Notes was a spotlight article on an existing program. Ultimately, all the adopters contributed materials describing their programs. When possible, snapshots of their staff were included and occasionally a photograph of the building that housed the program. The names and addresses of people who could be contacted for more information were printed at the end of each article. In this way, we hoped that the innovators would become focal points of the communication network, and that some interaction with staff at other hospitals would result. Another factor behind featuring a program as "program of the month" was to reward the innovators by providing their program with some exposure.

Occasionally adopters contributed articles directed at specific implementation issues. One such issue was community residents' resistance to the innovation, and one hospital presented its experience in defusing a neighborhood's effort to halt the implementation of a Lodge. Another article focused on

the role of the Lodge coordinator and presented a week's diary
of this person's activities.

In order to maximize the accessibility to innovators, a
directory of names, addresses, and phone numbers of all
adopters was printed in the third issue. As new Lodge
programs were developed, a supplemental directory was printed
in later issues. Again the hope was that readers would
contact the adopters for more information.

A total of eight issues of Lodge Notes were mailed prior
to gathering data relative to the experiment depicted in figure
7.1. Seventeen issues were published during the whole course
of the project.

The Questionnaire

A questionnaire was constructed to measure the impact of the
newsletter in three domains: innovation adoption, network
communication, and internal organizational processes.

The first factor, innovation adoption, tapped the following
variables: (1) interest in implementing the Lodge innovation;
(2) interest in receiving consultations or workshops; and (3)
number of deinstitutionalization programs adopted in the past
ten months. The first two items were Likert-type attitude
measures; the last was simply an open-ended question.

The second measurement domain was network communication; evaluated here was the extent to which individuals were
involved in innovation-related communication with the research
team, with the "innovators," with any other innovative programs, or with each other. Using an open-ended question
format, items were included in the following specific areas:
(1) the number of persons, if any, referred to the Michigan
State research team; (2) the number of Lodge adopters called,
written to, or visited; (3) the number of times they were
contacted for information about the Lodge innovation; (4) the
number of deinstitutionalization programs, other than the
Lodge, that had been called, written to, or visited; and (5)
the number of deinstitutionalization-related training sessions
they attended in the hospital setting.

The third area of measurement tapped various internal
organizational processes relevant to innovation. Several
Likert-type items gathered information on: (1) the amount of
discussion about the Lodge innovation; (2) the amount of
discussion about deinstitutionalization programs in general; and
(3) the existence of an advocate group for the Lodge innovation.

Additional questions were directed only to the experimental or control groups. The control group was asked
whether they would like to receive the newsletter, Lodge
Notes. The experimental group was asked several questions

related to its evaluation of the newsletter per se. Generally using a Likert-type multiple-option format, these questions assessed: (1) the general evaluation of the newsletter; (2) the extent to which the newsletter increased awareness about the innovation; (3) the extent to which the newsletter was perceived as a resource for the hospital work setting; (4) the extent to which the newsletter was used for effecting changes in the organization; (5) the final disposition of the newsletter, whether kept, passed on, or thrown away; and (6) the extent to which the newsletter was read.

For purposes of analysis, questionnaire data were aggregated at a given hospital. Mean scores across individual respondents were computed for each hospital. Staff from 47 of the 50 organizations responded to the survey. The individual response rate was generally quite poor (25 percent with an average of five questionnaires returned per organization), but it was difficult to parcel out how much of this was due to turnover, and the often uncertain fate of mailed questionnaires, as opposed to flat refusal to comply. At any rate, the response rate did not differ as a function of experimental condition, and for comparative purposes the data are worth considering.

Results

Comparative analyses

There were no significant differences between the experimental and control groups on any of the common variables (see tables 7.1-7.3). The newsletters did not encourage significantly more communication between organizations about the Lodge or other deinstitutionalization programs (table 7.2). It did not further staff interest in acquiring more information, or in adopting the Lodge or other deinstitutionalization innovation (table 7.1). It did not further discussion about programs within the organization (table 7.3). In short, this constitutes another set of data attesting to the negligible impact of print media.

Table 7.1. Impact of Lodge Notes on Innovation Adoption.

		e	df
Interest in Implementing Lodge Innovation	t = 10.16	ns	45
Interest in Receiving Consultations and Workshops	X^2 = .073	ns	1
# of Deinstitutionalization Programs Adopted	t = 7.86	ns	46

Table 7.2.   Impact of Lodge Notes on Network Communication.

	t	p	df
# of Persons Referred to Research Project	-19.43	ns	46
# of Lodge Adopters who were Called, Written, or Visited	-17.14	ns	46
# of Times Contacted about the Lodge Innovation	-18.98	ns	46
# of Deinstitutionalization Programs Visited, Written to, or Called	-13.10	ns	46
# of Training Sessions Attended on Deinstitutionalization	-2.25	ns	46

Table 7.3.   Impact of Lodge Notes on Internal Organizational Processes.

		p	df
Discussion about the Lodge Innovation	t = 2.75	ns	46
Discussion about Deinstitutionalization Programs	t = 12.34	ns	46
Existence of an Advocate Group for the Lodge Innovation	X^2 = .004	ns	1

Descriptive analysis

Given the lack of effect of the experimental Newsletter condition on the dependent variables, examining the same
variables and disregarding condition was felt to be instructive.
Percentages of responses for both experimental and control
group staff were computed.
   In the innovation adoption measurement area, 40 percent
of the staff indicated an interest in receiving further consultation or workshops about the innovation in response to an
open-ended question.   When asked about interest in implementation, however, the distribution of responses on a Likert
scale of no interest to a great deal of interest is more disap-
pointing, as shown in table 7.4.   Taken together, these two
items indicate that staff are perhaps always interested in a
workshop, but are understandably less enthusiastic about
committing themselves to work beyond the call of duty.

Table 7.4.   Interest in Implementing the Lodge Innovation.

A great deal	14.7%
Pretty much	14.3%
Some	20.4%
A little	17.1%
None	33.5%

Data are also available that relate to the network issues initially considered in the previous chapter. Based on these aggregated data, a strong argument can be made that hospital staff do not communicate very much across organizations, at least about the Lodge innovation or related programs. Table 7.5 depicts the frequency of such interorganizational exchanges across a variety of topics. The adopters were not reaching out to disseminate the program, nor did the non-adopters solicit help from the adopters. Although the newsletter was coordinated by the research project, the project staff received few referrals. Overwhelmingly (71.1 percent), organizations were not in contact with other organizations.

Table 7.5. Communication Network.

	Percent of organizations with yes responses
1. Contacted by other hospitals about the Lodge	1.2
2. Referred others to the research project	4.8
3. Personally contacted others about deinstitutionalization programs	13.7
4. Personally contacted Lodge adopters	9.2
5. No, or no response	71.1

When asked about the degree of internal discussion about the Lodge program, the respondents also indicated that there was very litle discussion in the hospital at large. Specifically, only 4 percent indicated that there was "a great deal of" or "much" discussion of the Lodge program. When asked about discussions of deinstitutionalization programs in general, 41 percent responded that there was either "a great deal of" or "much" discussion about deinstitutionalization programs. There was a difference in the degree of discussion about Lodge programs versus discussion about the general notion of deinstitutionalization. It is easier perhaps to promote discussion about abstract issues versus specific practices and programs.

When asked specifically about workshops, speakers, and training sessions on deinstitutionalization, approximately 27 percent of the respondents indicated that they had attended some training sessions on deinstitutionalization. There was more emphasis on seeking solutions to problems through training sessions than through visits to, or talks with staff from, programs that actually existed. These data can be interpreted as also supporting the notion of locally-inspired innovation.

Interest in receiving lodge notes

In answer to the question on whether they would like to receive the newsletter, 69 percent of the control group staff replied in the affirmative. Everyone likes to receive some mail.

Readers' general evaluation of the newsletter

It will be recalled that staff in the experimental condition were queried about their evaluation of such aspects of the newsletter as format, content, and utility. The first question involved the general response to the total newsletter. More than 75 percent of the group felt at least moderately positive about the newsletter, although a cynical analyst might surmise that most people would be "moderately positive" about anything that didn't cost them much. Table 7.6 lists the various ways in which the newsletter was seen as beneficial. It seemed that the newsletter was fairly effective in increasing awareness about the innovation, but was not as powerful in helping to identify problems, increasing desire to learn, or motivating follow-through on leads. The newsletter was used to some extent for proposing new practices, although it did not specifically stimulate change in organizational process.

Table 7.6. The Newsletter's Use:
A Rank Order from High to Low Use

Building Awareness about the Innovation	% Responses
1. Increasing awareness of resource availability	47.7
2. Helped identify problems and needs	19.3
3. Stimulated desire to learn	13.6
3. Motivated to follow-through on some leads	4.5

Resource for Work	
1. Proposing new practices	20.5
2. Use as a teaching device	6.8
3. Developing research proposal	1.1

For Changing the Organization	
1. Change in established practice	2.3
2. Start new practice	1.1

On a more basic level, we also wanted to determine how much of the material was read. The breakdown was as follows: don't read, 4.5 percent; skim, 40.4 percent; read part of it, 15.7 percent, read most of it, 39.3 percent. Indicative of how the newsletter was valued was how people disposed of it after reading it: 39.9 percent said they threw it away; 19.7 percent said they saved it for reference; and 34.8 percent passed it on to others.

SUMMARY AND IMPLICATIONS

The results of this experiment parallel much in the innovation processes literature. The dissemination of written materials, once again, appears to do very little in promoting behavioral changes in respondents. In this case, not only did the newsletter fail to promote innovation adoption, it had little effect on interorganizational or intraorganizational peer-to-peer communications. In a practical sense, the exercise was a failure. Nonetheless, these data do have important policy implications despite their redundancy with earlier findings (e.g., Fairweather, Sanders, and Tornatzky, 1974). At many levels of government, there are still attempts to disseminate information about, and to promote implementation of, "exemplary" social innovations through the use of printed materials. Government agencies, to a significant degree, are fueled by paper - guidelines, regulations, memoes, manuals, and the like. These data would indicate that unless such activities are coupled with more interpersonally intense interaction and sufficiently powerful incentives, the likelihood of effecting change is small. The role of printed media in this context seems to be to promote a very low level of awareness and passive interest in innovation.

8 El Dorado: A Case Study of Bureaucratic Entrepreneurship

Not all change is planned, predictable, or part of a well-orchestrated dissemination effort. This chapter describes an example of indigenously inspired diffusion in which the research team's role consisted primarily of being in the right place at the right time. There has always been considerable interest in the role of top administrators in the implementation of an innovation. What follows is a case study of the efforts of two top level administrators to diffuse the Lodge innovation in their own state.

Mental health systems, like most public bureaucracies, are usually responsible to some central administrative agency. In the case of state mental hospitals, that agency is usually the state department of mental health. Although administrative staff at mental hospitals have a great deal of flexibility and autonomy, they rely on policy and administrative directives emanating from the state central office. This does not mean that a superintendent or chief of staff at a hospital cannot decide to do something innovative; we have shown in a number of cases that this is possible. It does mean that by going ahead and innovating on his or her own, the hospital administrator takes on a risk since the innovation may not be as successful as predicted. Failure may have negative consequences for the hospital administrator, such as loss of influence, reprimands, or sanctions from the central office. It is often simply safer for a hospital administrator to wait for a directive or suggestion from superiors in the central office before introducing change into the system. Administrators and staff often wish someone would tell them what to do in regard to changing something in their organization. We have run across numerous examples of superintendents who would refuse to allow us to present a workshop at their hospital unless we obtained approval from the state central office.

THE BUREAUCRATIC ENTREPRENEUR

The role of the central office administrator as a "gatekeeper" for innovation processes has been well described (Fairweather, Sanders, and Tornatzky, 1974). There are, however, other roles that administrators can perform with regard to innovations. If a high level bureaucrat becomes interested in an innovation, he or she can become its "champion." As an active advocate, the bureaucrat can mobilize resources and political support and can act as a leader throughout the implementation process. Lambright (1977) has elaborated a useful concept in his description of the bureaucratic entrepreneur in the context of state and local government innovations. Such an entrepreneur is able to mobilize "the minimum winning coalition" of adopters, implementers, clients, and suppliers needed for innovation, and to set the implementation process into action. This set of concepts is particularly appropriate for the El Dorado case study described in this chapter.

It is not clear what distinguishes a bureaucratic entrepreneur, in terms of motivation, demographics, or circumstances, from the rest of the bureaucratic mass. Obviously, interest in championing an innovation is a matter of willingness to take risks. While the bureaucrat may have been concerned about a particular problem for some time, it is likely necessary that some external stimulus exists to put the problem and possible solution on his or her immediate agenda. The external stimulus can assume the form of a threat, or some special circumstance or opportunity.

However, it is not enough for a bureaucracy to be stimulated by external threats or opportunities. Additional pressure and/or persuasion from inside the organization is necessary to promote the innovation beyond the thinking stage. Coalition building is of particular importance here for exerting pressure to move ahead with the implementation of the innovation. A group of interested decision makers and implementers must be convened and maintained to provide the necessary support for an innovation. However, the interests or preferences of the bureaucratic entrepreneur may not be the same as those of others within the agency, so a wide-ranging core of support is essential in order to convince others within the organization.

While service efficiency and cost efficiency appear to be the most important outcomes for an innovation, it is also likely that issues such as bureaucratic self-interest, professional values, necessities to adopt an innovation partially, and maintaining relationships with the suppliers of an innovation are all important predictors of whether an innovation will be implemented. To contend with these crosscurrents, entre-

preneurship requires a core of support that brings together
people with good technical skills and professional judgment as
well as good political skills. The coalition, or support group,
serves to present the innovation in terms that will appeal to
bureaucrats' self-interest and maintain good relationships with
the suppliers. The coalition, then, is vital to the success of
the innovation advocated by the bureaucratic entrepreneur.
One important note: as described by Lambright (1977), the
entrepreneur operates until incorporation of the innovation is
achieved, when the innovation becomes part of the routine
practice of the organization.

ROUTINIZATION OF THE INNOVATION

Yin (1978) has described in considerable richness the process
by which an innovation moves through various "passages and
cycles," until it is no longer perceived as new, but has
become an accepted part of organizational practice. Once an
innovation is introduced into an organization, it must be
routinized to a degree such that it is no longer perceived as a
novelty. The use of the innovation in the agency must be
seen as other than a special project, if the innovation is to go
beyond the stage where it is perceived and treated as a
temporary aberration on the part of a few marginal members of
the organization. Routinization is the process by which
innovations become part of standard practice.

The overall course of routinization, as described by Yin
(1978) occurs within three stages. First the innovation is
introduced, and attempts are made to interface the new
practice with existing ones. This is known as improvisation.
During the improvisation stage, the support group of adopters
and implementers is forged, and attempts are made to persuade
stakeholders that the innovation is in their best interests.
The second step involves moving beyond the novelty phase
into one that brings the innovation into the mainstream of the
organization's functions or practices. This process is called
expansion. In this way, the innovation loses its special
project connotation and begins to seem part of the core
services or practices of an organization. The final step in
routinization is the process by which the innovation is no
longer perceived as new. This is called disappearance.
Disappearance refers only to the removal of the "newness"
label. Through this three-step process, an innovation becomes
standard practice.

Within those three stages, a number of what Yin (1978)
calls cycles, or passages, usually occur. The former term
refers to changes that occur repeatedly during the lifetime of
the organization; the latter refers to changes that involve

transition from one organizational state to another. Once accomplished, a passage situation will not usually reappear. In contrast, cycles are repetitive events, often tied to the continuing turnover at time, personnel, and activities in the organization. For example, a budget-related passage might inovlve a transition from soft to hard money; a budget-related cycle would involve surviving one or more fiscal years. A personnel-related passage would involve creating job descriptions for individuals in the innovation program, and a personnel-related cycle would involve surviving employee turnover and promotion of key individuals. "The routinization of an innovation may be described in terms of its ability to negotiate several passages as well as its ability to survive a period of organizational cycles" (Yin, 1978, p. 46).

Steps Leading to Routinization

The discrete steps associated with an innovation's routinization are specific to the organization that incorporates the innovation. The adopting organization has to tailor the innovation so that it is compatible with the agency and gains the support of staff and administrators. There are, however, steps common to all routinizing efforts. First, the appropriate innovation skills and resources must be established within the organization. For example, a group of practitioners must be trained to use the innovation so that they can start using it right away. Second, the innovation must be integrated immediately into standard procedures. It must be integrated such that administration and staffing are not set up as if the innovation were a limited time special project. For example, if an innovation replaces an old practice, it will have to be integrated into the organizational system. This will do much to ensure its acceptance by staff and administration.

The Community Lodge is an example of an innovation that can be integrated into an organization. It is one of the "least restrictive" residential treatment alternatives available for the chronic mentally disabled. Often hospitals or mental health centers, which are ostensibly mandated to provide care for these populations, have little in the way of residential treatment alternatives. These agencies may send their patients to board-and-care homes that are too restrictive, or simply discharge them into the community, which is not restrictive enough. The Lodge, then, fills a gap left by these two alternatives. It may also replace the old practice of simply discharging the patients who are not capable of full, independent living in the community.

If the innovation is to take hold, it must be supported by agency practitioners. This support will occur in part if the innovation provides a new practice to a program in the

agency. The agency staff also have to be convinced that the
new practice is more effective than the old one, and the proof
has eventually to come from the staff's own experiences with
the innovation. However, as mentioned earlier, it is more
often self-interest rather than cost or service efficiency that
determines whether or not the innovation will be supported.
In the case of the Lodge, clinicians are told they have to give
up one-to-one therapy with the Lodge clients. In some
instances, therapy is so important to staff that they are
unwilling to give it up, regardless of its usefulness to their
clients; the Lodge is not perceived as serving staff's self-
interests. In organizations where such clinicians are numerous, or where they occupy top level administration positions,
the Lodge will neither take hold nor be routinized.
      Another very important condition leading to routinization
is the support of top agency administrators. Administrators
usually are essential to the decisions about whether or not to
adopt the innovation, or whether or not to make staff and
funds available. Again, however, it may be the self-interests
of the top level administrators that determine what will happen
to an innovation.

THE RELATIONSHIP BETWEEN BUREAUCRATIC ENTREPRENEURSHIP AND ROUTINIZATION: THE CASE OF EL DORADO

The point to be illustrated by the ensuing case study is that
routinization and entrepreneurship are crucially interdependent
processes. The efforts of a bureaucratic entrepreneur
ultimately must be directed toward the goal of routinization.
The goal of innovating is to improve organizational practice,
and if an implemented innovation does not maintain its fragile
hold on life, then the gains accrued to clients will be negated.
Initiation and partial implementation of an innovation are not
sufficient unto themselves.
      The point is that a bureaucratic entrepreneur from
central office with strong authority may easily be able to
introduce an innovation into a system. The entrepreneur may
be effective in forming a winning coalition to forge ahead with
the innovation, and the innovation may prove itself effective,
but unless the innovation becomes routinized, the efforts of
the bureaucratic entrepreneur will be for naught. Specifically, the innovation must be seen as part of the agency's
core responsibilities and services, and it must have continuing
top administrative support and organizational status if it is to
survive. The cycles and passages described by Yin must be
successfully accomplished.

The remainder of this chapter describes a case study in which a bureaucratic entrepreneur was found, and successful efforts were made to introduce the innovation into a state system. Whether or not the innovation was fully routinized is problematic.

The Historical Context

In the previous Lodge dissemination research (Fairweather, et al., 1974), virtually every state and federal psychiatric hospital in the country was approached and asked to implement the Community Lodge program. In the current research, while considerably fewer hospitals were contacted, all had been contacted during the earlier study. This gave us a good historical perspective on a particular hospital's or state's interest in the Lodge innovation. A state which we shall refer to as El Dorado is one case in point.

El Dorado, circa 1975-79, was a good site for implementation of this mental health innovation. Although there had been some shift of patients from the hospital to the community during the 1960s, there had been a few successful efforts to develop community treatment programs that were as demonstrably successful as the Lodge. Although patient populations had shifted, monies, for the most part, still remained earmarked for state hospital in-patient programs. As a result, there had been no apparent dollar savings resulting from community programming. This led to a continuing quandary about community care in El Dorado. The bulk of funding (90 percent) for mental health in El Dorado continued to be directed to the state institutions. El Dorado would seem to be a state in which there would be a felt need for the type of innovation being disseminated.

In the earlier Fairweather, Sanders, and Tornatzky (1974) dissemination study, eight hospitals in the state of El Dorado had been approached: Kindly State Hospital, Sympathy State Hospital, Harmony State Hospital, Tranquil State Hospital, Restful State Hospital, Weal State Hospital, Benign State Hospital, and Amenable State Hospital. Kindly State Hospital wasn't interested in the program at that time because, as stated by their contact person, "a mental health center is being set up." Amenable State Hospital also flatly declined the offer of consultation assistance. Here is an excerpt from their rejection letter:

> We find that, at this time, we just do not have a building that we could devote for this purpose.

> We are in the process of trying to decentralize the hospital and find ourselves much occupied.

Benign State Hospital provided a somewhat different rationale
for refusing technical assistance in 1971:

> The general feeling among the majority of our
> hospital staff was that a program such as yours
> would necessitate the discontinuation or dilution of
> several other programs currently being developed
> within the hospital, as well as in the community.
> Further, it appeared that many of the ideas pre-
> sented to us are, although in modified forms,
> already part of our hospital's treatment philosophy
> and practice.

Two other hospitals, Harmony and Sympathy, provided similar
reasons for refusing consultation assistance.

Weal and Restful State Hospitals were more interested in
receiving consultation, but 14 months later they were both still
involved in "planning" to implement the program. As subsequent correspondence proved fruitless, contact with the
hospitals was terminated.

One hospital did make a definite effort to implement the
innovation: Tranquil State Hospital asked for and received four
days of on-site consultation. As a result of these contacts,
Tranquil State Hospital adopted portions of the innovation and
was able to start a modified version of the Lodge program.
However, the implementation effort ceased within a few months
after start-up and was never heard from again. The reasons
for continuance were obscure.

In summary, when the current diffusion study began
seven years later, there was no trace of any Community Lodge
innovation activity in the state of El Dorado. During Phase I
(pp. 40 to 56) of the current study, four hospitals were part
of the sample and were again contacted: Benign, Sympathy,
Harmony, and Kindly State Hospitals.

Benign State Hospital again declined implementation with
the following reason:

> The Executive Planning Committee decided that
> there are presently too many priorities for the
> hospital which would not allow adequate time for the
> planning and preparation necessary to implement this
> program.

Harmony State Hospital also declined because: (1) the in-
patient population was not perceived as appropriate for the
innovation; (2) support might be more easily obtained if the
researchers worked through the local mental health center; and
(3) the staff were not interested. Kindly State Hospital
wouldn't even talk to the researchers without explicit approval
from the central office, and Sympathy State Hospital was

interested only in receiving "more information," not in consultation assistance.

Thus, nearly ten years after our first contact with El Dorado's state hospitals, little had been accomplished. In two instances, it was clear that the hospital superintendents would take no risks and wanted explicit approval from central office. In the other instances, while there may have been interest in the innovation, there was no one to take the lead and push for implementation.

Being in the Right Place at the Right Time

About a year after our last Phase I contact with any El Dorado state hospital, the research team received a call from a middle level administrator in the state department of mental health at the state capital. The caller wanted to know more in general about the Lodge program, and specifically where the program was currently operating and what steps a hospital would have to take in starting such a program. Interestingly, the inquiry came, not as a result of our contact with the El Dorado state hospitals, but as a result of the administrator's conversation with someone who had been on a panel discussion with a member of the research team at a professional meeting a few months before. Informal, serendipitous interaction between peers strikes again.

At the time of the telephone inquiry, the researchers were heavily involved in Phase II of the research (chapter 5), and were spending a great deal of time conducting consultations at the hospitals in their sample. As an immediate referral, it was suggested that the El Dorado administrator call the director of an ongoing Lodge program in Minnesota. Coincidentally, the Minnesota Lodge Program was sponsoring a conference on Lodges and their implementation later that month. The El Dorado administrator, his supervisor, and one person from Tranquil State Hospital attended the conference. At the conference, they became very excited about the possibility of starting such a program. After seeing the program in operation and discussing it with the adopters, they returned to El Dorado determined to implement the innovation. (The experience here was instrumental in deciding to implement the site visit experiment described in chapter 9.) The El Dorado Department of Mental Health arranged for staff from the Minnesota Lodge to consult with staff at Tranquil State Hospital, and to advise them how to start the program. Interested staff from Amenable and Sympathy State Hospital also attended that consultation.

After the initial consultation, the administrator from the El Dorado central office made numerous phone calls to our project staff requesting information on other programs that had succeeded, programs that had failed, and background on implementation efforts that had been attempted in El Dorado. In the meantime, staff from Sympathy and Amenable State Hospitals were also expressing an interest in joining Tranquil State Hospital in implementing a Lodge program.

Three months later, one of our research team was serendipitously planning a trip to a nearby state and offered to spend a few extra days in El Dorado to consult with staff at Amenable, Sympathy, and Tranquil State Hospitals. Since the cost was minimal, the research project picked up the consultant's expenses. As a result of this consultation, Amenable, Sympathy, and Tranquil State Hospitals became very actively involved in starting the program. Over the next six months, the researcher again visited Amenable, Sympathy, and Tranquil State Hospitals individually and consulted with them on program implementation. Since it was necessary for the consultant to spend a great deal of time in the state, and trips in the area were not forthcoming, the El Dorado Department of Mental Health subsequently began paying the consultant's expenses. This began a series of consultations which led to the implementation of the Lodge program in three hospitals.

Role of the Bureaucratic Entrepreneur

At the time of the consultant's second visit, it became clear that the middle level administrator, who had initially contacted us, was receiving a great deal of support from his supervisor, a Deputy Commissioner within the central office. The Deputy Commissioner and the administrator had, in effect, become the bureaucratic entrepreneurs. Together the administrator and the Deputy Commissioner had been able to work out a supportive coalition that was interested in starting the Lodge program.

For example, they politicked state and local level department of vocational rehabilitation staff and convinced them to attend the early consultations. The department of vocational rehabilitation subsequently became an important source of start-up money for the Lodge. Specifically, funds were made available for room and board, work adjustment, and vocational training for patients in the program. This financial backing came in spite of that department's lack of precedent for dealing with mental health clients in groups. Normally the department would not fund the kind of client who is a member of the Lodge because he or she is not likely to become "independent" in the strictest sense of the term.

The central office innovators also had to forge several interorganizational arrangements within the mental health system. In El Dorado the hospitals historically had total and exclusive responsibility for running in-patient programs. In contrast, community centers had responsibility, though neither total nor exclusive, for running out-patient programs. The three adopting hospitals, and the community centers to which they related organizationally, had initially agreed to work simultaneously on the in-hospital and the community program components respectively. While the hospital was setting up the in-hospital group ward, the community centers were to make arrangements for finding a residence and starting a business. When the centers and the hospitals cooperated in this manner, implementation moved very quickly. When the two organizations didn't cooperate, implementation hit a snag. At Sympathy State Hospital, the community center began to interfere with rather than help in the establishment of the Lodge. The central office administrators eventually had to intervene and convince the local staff to implement the program without the support of the community center. In a memo sent to her superiors to recommend implementing the Lodge without the help of the community center, the central office innovator stated:

> I want to emphasize that this is not an attempt at a "power grab," and there is no intent to push the Community Center out of the picture. I still think that the Center can make a positive contribution to the project. However, we must face the reality that there is a chance that the Center will choose not to participate, and progress toward development of a community lodge has been far from satisfactory to date. Concern for the Fairweather patient group forces us into action.

The administrator and the Deputy Commissioner perceived themselves as "catalysts":

> Although the central office has ultimate responsibility for the state hospitals, the central office role has to be one of providing gentle, prodding support . . . As central office personnel, we cannot operate programs directly or even "order" that specific programs be implemented. What we can do is provide information about good programs which make sense, and help create conditions under which some extremely capable field personnel can function more effectively. (Lodge Notes, January, 1978)

Compare that self-description with Lambright's (1977) analysis that bureaucratic entrepreneurs "build necessary coalitions among adopters, implementers, clients, and suppliers that make it possible for local public organizations to adopt and use new technology" (p. 37).

This catalyst role includes a number of functions: organizing consultants; bringing together principal parties involved in starting the program; legitimizing the innovation; and trouble-shooting and problem-solving difficulties that arise during the implementation process. The organizing and trouble-shooting efforts were important as a means of training hospital staff in the use of the innovation and getting them to begin using it as soon as possible. The legitimizing attempts were a means of getting top level administrative support.

Successful Implementation - Finally

After over ten years of dissemination efforts in El Dorado, Lodges were finally adopted and implemented at three state hospitals: Sympathy State Hospital, Amenable State Hospital, and Tranquil State Hospital. Below is a description of the Lodge at Sympathy State Hospital:

> A look inside the Fairweather Lodge reveals a special family. No, they're not a talkative bunch, but the visitor senses an underlying and unifying support. Anthony rests an arm around Emmitt Lee and quietly says, "He's been just like a father to me." During dinner, Irwin praises Fred, "You know, you make darn good enchiladas." Throughout the day, hundreds of such seemingly negligible comments can be heard. Having a family to share, support, and care for you is what Fairweather is all about. (Fawcett, 1978)

Amenable State Hospital describes their Lodge:

> After several delays, the Lodge members spent the first night in their home November 17. The level of excitement and energy was high when the group returned from work, and staff held a welcome home party for them. (Lodge Notes, January, 1978)

Tranquil State Hospital also describes their Lodge:

> The group moved into three adjacent apartments on November 18. Two apartments are used for sleeping, and the middle apartment is used for cooking, group meetings, and recreation. The Lodge is located close to a shopping center, library, bus lines, and the community mental health center. The group is employed by a janitorial company which employed them 6 weeks prior to their move into the community. (Lodge Notes, January, 1978)

Each of the three hospitals had an in-hospital group ward and two Lodges in the community. All three had been previously contacted by the research staff either in the first or second diffusion study. However, prior to the push from the central office innovators, little or nothing had been accomplished.

Having established programs at three hospitals, the central office entrepreneurs decided to work with two additional hospitals. Restful State Hospital set aside a building and assigned staff to implement a small group ward. As of this writing, staff there are still moving toward implementation of the Lodge. Weal State Hospital was chosen as a demonstration site for a possible research grant, and the Lodge was implemented there.

In the implementation of the program at Weal State Hospital, there were several ominous forebodings. During the initial planning stages, the program coordinator showed the consultant and the central office innovators the proposed on-grounds building for the hospital portion of the program. Most of the hospital buildings in that institution had been remodeled extensively and were an example of model psychiatric facilities. The building that was to be the site of the Lodge program was one of the few that had not been remodeled. In his tour of the building, the program coordinator was careful to point out the rat droppings in the closet, the broken sewer pipes over the kitchen, and the lack of the air conditioning. The tour was abruptly ended, and the Depty Commissioner went directly to the superintendent's office for a meeting. By the end of the day, the new program site was to be in one of the air conditioned, remodeled buildings. It is clear that, had the Deputy Commissioner not demanded another building, the program would never have been implemented. Despite their successes in the other three settings, the facilitative role of the bureaucratic entrepreneur was still needed.

Innovative programs such as the Lodge had often had trouble getting a hearing in the El Dorado systems. This is evident from the fruitless efforts of the two previous dissemination projects.

The Issue of Routinization: Exit the Entrepreneurs

As discussed earlier, once an innovation is implemented, it has to be perceived as part of the organization's core system of services in order to survive. If the program is regarded as a special project, or has not become routinized in Yin's terms, its future is debatable. For example, the program at Amenable State Hospital was still viewed by administrators as a special project. The chief of staff had initially agreed to setting up the program as a special one to two year project. However, the cooperation between the community center and the hospital has been exemplary, and had been instrumental in continuing the program to date. Recently, however, the hospital census has been increasing to the point where many of the units are presently overcrowded. The in-hospital group ward staff at Amenable State Hospital are very much aware that they have more staff and more empty beds than any other unit in the hospital. This has meant that their program has been scrutinized by the administration. It is not clear at this point whether the top administrators see this as a part of the core services of the program or as a special project. The situation was similar at the other two sites.

It was at this juncture that a rather ominous event occurred. After approximately two years of program advocacy, both of the bureaucratic entrepreneurs left the state for other positions. Although three hospitals had successfully implemented the program, the future of the innovation has survived a number of organizational cycles and negotiated several organizational passages. From table 8.1 we see that the Lodge programs in El Dorado have survived an initial round of organizational cycles. It is also clear, however, that the programs have had some difficulty with organizational passages. In this particular setting, the bureaucratic entrepreneur was most helpful in enabling the innovation to survive organizational cycles. The tasks of routinization and complete incorporation, had not been finished prior to the principal actors leaving the scene. Looking at the various cycles and passages, it would appear that while the innovations have stood the initial test of temporal survival, their "organizational legitimacy" - in the form of bureaucratized and concretized procedures - has not been established.

Since the product champions' departure, other stakeholders within the central office have gradually begun to recoup some of the authority and territory they perceived they had lost. Specifically, the community centers had perceived that the Lodge program, as currently implemented, had resulted in some loss in responsibility for them. Although seen as successful, the Lodge program was also seen as a program which competes with community centers for service delivery, resources, and attention. This problem occurred partly in response to the situation at Sympathy State Hospital, which had used a nonprofit corporation to run the Lodge instead of the community center. These territorial moves could easily affect the ability of the program to survive future organizational cycles, or to move it through the remaining passages at the three settings.

Six months after the bureaucratic entrepreneurs had left the scene, another consultation was held at Weal State Hospital. It was apparent that some changes had occurred in the interim. This was clearly manifested by the absence of the

Table 8.1. Organizational Passages and
Cycles Related to Routinization.

	Amenable State Hospital	Sympathy State Hospital	Tranquil State Hospital
CYCLES			
Start up funds made available	yes	yes	yes
Staff made available to implement program	yes	yes	yes
Job skills taught at training sessions	yes	yes	yes
Survives personnel turnover	yes	yes	yes
Survives annual budget cycles	yes	yes	yes
Key personnel promoted up through organization	no	no	no
PASSAGES			
Program support shifts from soft to hard money	yes	yes	yes
Functions become part of job descriptions or prerequisites for similar positions throughout organization	no	no	no
Program job skills become recognized as part of professional role of staff	no	no	no
Program is given official status within the organization	no	yes	unclear
Program becomes part of institution's written statement of services provided	no	no	no
Regulations and procedures modified to accommodate staff roles in program	no	no	no

hospital's previous gracious hospitality. The consultant and
the central office staff who flew in to attend the consultation
had always had a hospital car at their disposal. During this
trip, however, the assistant superintendent chided the central
office staff about driving too much and warned that future
requests for a car might be denied.

The new role of the central office personnel had changed.
These new staff did not see themselves as catalysts, nor were
they creating conditions to help hospital personnel function
more effectively as did their predecessors. The mental health
center and Weal Hospital were not getting along, and the
sympathies of the central office staff were in support of the
mental health center, despite the fact that they were from the
institutions division rather than the center division. Due to
some administrative changes instituted by the new staff, the
cooperation and support of the mental health center were now
crucial to the development of the Lodge. The mental health
center staff, however, were neither cooperating nor supporting
the Lodge. The program director continually came up with
excuses for not moving toward implementation and the central
office staff were largely ineffective in doing something about
it.

The Weal Hospital program will have to survive on the
basis of the commitment that local staff and hospital administrators have for it, and its eventual movement through other
organizational passages. Whether or not this role change in
central office will effect other programs in El Dorado is not
clear at the time of this writing. Clearly, it will be more
difficult for a hospital to move through various passages given
the hospitals' reluctance to change without central office
support, and given their territorial concerns with the mental
health centers.

Conclusions

A person in a position of authority in a bureaucracy, given
the interest and the opportunity, can champion an innovation.
The person can develop a support group and identify and
develop appropriate skills and resources to help the program's
implementation, but, if the innovation does not become a
perceived part of the core agency practice, receives no
continuing administrative support, or fails to negotiate the full
tortuous path of routinization, the long-term success may be
meteoric.

The implications of this case study are many. On the one
hand, the El Dorado experience is a reconfirmation of the
notion that a few motivated people can work wonders in
reforming a bureaucratic system, but the experience also
illustrates the inertia of such systems, and the necessity for
the immediate institutionalization of fragile innovations.

The implications for subsequent research are twofold. First, it appears that work needs to be divided toward possible identifying potential "bureaucratic entrepeneurs" in orgainzation system. If such work could avoid the morass of past studies in leadership, and identify a finite number of descriptors of such persons, the benefit could be considerable. Some efforts in promoting innovations in state and local government have focused on the concept of "capacity-building," or the creation of the impetus for change at the user level. It would seem that the highlighting of the role at the bureaucratic entrepeneur would be of considerable assistance here.

Secondly, strategies of change agentry and consultation need perhaps to focus on issues of routinization, and stabilization of hard-won gains. Our recurrent preoccupation with an "innovation bias" (Rogers, 1975) has hampered this development. The concept of incremental social change rests partially on the premise that improvements, and successful innovations, will not be reversed by subsequent events. Unfortunately, the prospect of "reinventing the wheel" is all too real in public service agencies dealing with complex social technologies.

9 Site Visits and Innovation Processes: An Experiment *

Some stocktaking may be in order as we look retrospectively at the previous three chapters. It does appear, on the basis of the El Dorado case study, and from supporting literature, that local change agentry can be a powerful tool in innovation adoption and implementation. However, it also appears, on the basis of the chapter 6 network study, that there is little peer-to-peer communication about innovations that transcends regional or organizational boundaries. It also seems that attempts to facilitate this type of communication through printed media are not terribly effective.

If it is desirable to promote transfer of social technology between indigenous innovators and potential users, how can this process be facilitated? This chapter describes an attempt to enhance peer-to-peer knowledge transfer and technical assistance that relies significantly on some common-sensical notions. The idea that "seeing is believing" is a well-worn American truism. It implies that actually seeing something in operation should help to convince one that the thing being seen is real or effective. The study discussed in this chapter approached the dissemination of the Lodge innovation from that perspective. It was an experimental test of an agricultural extension technique transplanted to a public service bureaucracy setting.

THE PERSISTENT PROBLEM OF UNCERTAINTY

As has already been noted frequently, one of the major problems for public bureaucracies such as mental hospitals is

---

*This chapter was written by Mitchell Fleischer.

164

the fact that they are not organized in ways that enable them
to adopt and implement innovations easily. Bureaucracies are
not structured to deal with the uncertainty involved in the
process of innovating. As a variety of contingency theorists
have noted over the past 20 years, heavily bureaucratized
organizations have elaborate sets of rules and hierarchies, well
suited for stable environments and routine tasks, but difficult
to apply to nonroutine tasks such as change (Litwak, 1961).
One approach to this problem has been to attempt to change
the structure and system of relations within organizations in
order to make them more amenable to change. This is ex-
emplified by the Organization Development approach employed
in the Phase II experiment.

There are other approaches that could conceivably impact
on uncertainty. March and Simon (1958) define uncertainty in
terms of knowledge about alternatives. They state that an
alternative is uncertain if one lacks a conception of the
probabilities of positive or negative outcomes that might arise
from the implementation of the alternative. The probabilities
are unknown because either the outcomes, or the utility of the
outcomes, are unknown. Simplistically, it would seem that one
way to reduce uncertainty about an innovation would be to
provide more knowledge about it, but it is not enough merely
to convey information about an innovation. The earlier
Fairweather, Sanders, and Tornatzky (1974) study of the
effects of brochures and do-it-yourself manuals showed that
information alone, in the absence of a social contact, does not
produce very much change. To paraphrase a more learned
student of communication (McLuhan, 1964), the social context
is the message, at least in regard to innovation-related
information.

Reducing Uncertainty Through Personal Contact

One technique that could provide such a different quality of
information would more directly involve peer-to-peer communication. Sending prospective adopters to visit the site of
an ongoing innovative program could be a way to accomplish
this. This technique would have a number of advantages, not
the least of which would be the opportunity for the site visitor
to interact, on an informal basis, with a number of his or her
peers who are actually operating the program which is the
focus of the innovation decision. The staff of such a progarm
should be perceived as having more legitimacy and expertise
than a consultant, who is often perceived as an outsider.
Much of what might happen in this setting is akin to a social
comparison process (Festinger, 1954), in which the visitor
might come to perceive that establishing the innovation is, in
fact, possible. A redefinition of social reality might occur.

An important point is that an innovation such as the Community Lodge must be adopted and implemented by an organization, or by a group within an organization, rather than by an individual. A site visit should be particularly advantageous in an organizational setting. This is because the site visitor could not only become an advocate for the program, but could also attain a more meaningful insight into the organizational dynamics of implementation. Because of the visitor's linkages to the hospital and its culture, he or she should be a more credible change agent than an outside consultant. Theoretically, an informal adoption group might form around such an advocate, something which Fairweather, Sanders, and Tornatzky (1974) found essential for actual implementation of the Lodge. An implicit hypothesis of this site visit experiment is that site visitors might become bureaucratic entrepreneurs (Lambright, 1977) as a result of their experience and site visit revelations.

Relevant Literature on Site Visits

While the notion of a site visit makes good theoretical sense as well as good common sense, there have been few methodologically respectable tests of its effectiveness in promoting innovation adoption and implementation in a bureaucratic organization. The few tests that have been conducted have either had little relevance to the problem at hand (e.g., individual adopters in an agricultural setting), or have been inconclusive in their results.

The most widespread use of the site visit technique has undeniably been in agricultural extension work, involving the use of demonstration farms. When one farmer in an area has been convinced to pilot a new product or technique, other farmers are given the opportunity to visit the demonstration farm and talk with the farmer. This is recognized as a very effective technique, although its applicability beyond the agricultural setting is difficult to determine. Of particular relevance is the fact that agricultural extension work has usually focused on individual farmers, rather than on anything similar to a cumbersome service bureaucracy.

Malcolm Richland (1965) has tested the use of site visits, or in his words, "traveling seminars," in the area of education. The "seminars" were made up of groups of educators who traveled to different schools that had set up exemplary programs. In his follow-up a year later, he found that school systems involved in the visits had adopted more innovations during that year than had schools in a control group. However, Richland was not attempting to influence his educators to adopt a specific innovation; his purpose was to make them "more innovative" generally. There was little attention paid to the degree and dynamics of actual implementation.

Edward Glaser, of the Human Interaction Research Institute, has also done some work in this area. In one study (Glaser and Ross, 1971), an attempt was made to persuade Community Mental Health Centers to adopt a specific treatment program by means of a site visit arrangement. Unfortunately, no adoption of the program took place, rendering their results somewhat inconclusive.

In a more recent study, Larsen, Artunian, and Finley (1974) used site visits in an attempt to make Community Mental Health Centers more innovative once again in a general sense. They used a number of experimental conditions to test the relative effects of written materials, site visits, and consultation visits, but found no significant differences between conditions as to innovativeness. Thus, except for Richland's study, the results of site visit experiments have been weak at best. It seems that the technique has considerable theoretical backing and intuitive appeal, but little empirical support as yet.

Experimental Hypotheses

In this study, a number of hypotheses were developed as to the effects that a site visit ought to have on a mental hospital and its staff. These were divided into three categories. The first two hypotheses were a check on the basic process involved. If the site visit is to have any effect at all, people at the "home" hospital must talk to the site visitor, who, it is hoped, is now an advocate for the innovation. Thus the first two hypotheses were:

1. The site visit would increase the amount of general discussion about the Lodge program among hospital staff;
2. As a result of the site visit, there would be an increase in the intensity of communication directed toward the opinion leader(s) in the organization.

In the above discussion, it was suggested that reduction of uncertainty about the innovation may be an intervening variable between initial awareness of an innovation and its actual adoption and implementation. This yielded a number of intervening variable hypotheses:

3. A site visit would reduce the amount of uncertainty staff felt concerning the effectiveness of the Lodge innovation;
4. A site visit would reduce the amount of uncertainty staff felt concerning the feasibility of the Lodge innovation;
5. A site visit would reduce the amount of uncertainty staff felt concerning their how-to knowledge about implementing the Lodge innovation;

6. A site visit would result in more favorable staff attitudes toward the Lodge innovation.

Finally, there was the principal dependent variable hypothesis dealing with the issue of change:

7. A site visit would result in a greater degree of implementation of the Lodge innovation, and in behaviors directed to that end.

METHOD

What follows is a description of the experiment that was performed to test these hypotheses. Basically, the study involved a comparison of one group of hospitals, that sent staff on a site visit, with a control group of hospitals, whose staff did not make a site visit.

Sample

The sample consisted of 24 state hospitals in the northeast quarter of the United States. They were chosen because they were omitted from the sample of 108 in the study described in chapter 3, and because they were within approximately 1000 miles of East Lansing, Michigan (see figure 9.1). Of the 44 hospitals that were called initially called and offered an introductory workshop on the Lodge innovation, 24 agreed to: (1) have the workshop; and (2) send a staff member on an expense-paid trip to visit a Lodge, should that opportunity be made available. In effect, all hospitals were volunteers for both cells. Since information about these hospitals' previous willingness to change was available (see p. 39), they were matched on the basis of that change score, and then randomly assigned to the site visit and control conditions (see figure 9.2).

Procedure

The study had four operational phases: approach, persuasion, site visit, and follow-up.

Approach and persuasion

In the approach phase, a letter and two brochures describing the program were sent to the hospital superintendent. The letter said that a call would be forthcoming, in which an offer

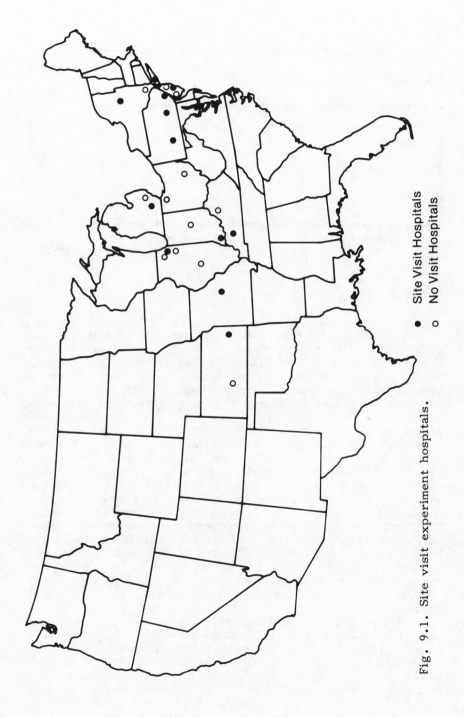

Fig. 9.1. Site visit experiment hospitals.

• Site Visit Hospitals
○ No Visit Hospitals

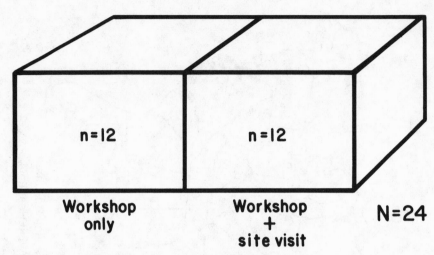

Fig. 9.2.   Design of the site visit experiment.

of free training and consultation assistance in establishing the
Lodge would be made.   During the call, the project was
described, and the superintendent was asked if the hospital
would like to receive the workshop presentation.   Often a
decision was made immediately; sometimes it took a few weeks.

The workshop, of course, was the "persuasion" phase of
the intervention.   This lasted one day, and its content and
format approximately paralleled the workshop described in
chapter 3.   It was open to both interested hospital staff and
representatives of community agencies.   A total of 606 individuals attended the workshops across all 24 hospitals.   The
workshop had two parts: a morning session and an afternoon
session.   The morning session consisted of a two-hour talk,
complete with a movie and a slide presentation, and a question-answer period.   After the question-answer period, there
was some discussion about the kinds of assistance that could
be provided to the hospital.   These included written materials,
that were handed out at the end of the day, free telephone
consultation, and free consultation visits to the hospital, if the
ward part of the program was set up and operated for at least
60 days.

Those hospitals in the Site Visit condition were also
offered an expense-paid site visit to a hospital with an ongoing
Lodge program.   The afternoon session consisted of an
extended discussion about the mechanics of setting up a small
group ward.   At the conclusion of that discussion, the
participants were asked to fill out a questionnaire.   Also at
the end of the workshop, groups in the site visit condition

were asked to choose one person to make the site visit. In about half the cases, a person was selected immediately; in the rest, the decision was made within two weeks.

Site visit

The third operational phase of the experiment was the site visit itself. Obviously, there was no activity during this phase for the Control condition hospitals. In the Site Visit group, one member of the hospital staff was sent on an expense-paid visit to an exemplary Lodge program in Minnesota. The initial Lodge had been set up in 1970, and five additional Lodges had been established since then. The Minnesota staff were an enthusiastic group, and were quick to accept the idea of hosting the site visits. A schedule was prepared for activities during the visits and was followed quite closely. Three to six visitors, each from different hospitals, participated in the three visits.

During a typical two-day site visit, the visitors had the opportunity to meet with staff from the small group ward and Lodge programs, to see and meet with patients and residents of the programs, to attend various meetings, to visit Lodge residences, and to watch Lodge members at work in their places of business. Before the visitors left, they filled out a brief questionnaire, which included questions on the similarity of the hospital in Minnesota with their home institution, and on their feelings about the visit itself.

Follow-up

Follow-up activities took place for over a year after the workshop. During the initial follow-up, three months after the workshop, all participants in both Site Visit and Control conditions were mailed a questionnaire, 365 of which were returned. At three, six, nine, and thirteen months after the workshop, our contact at the hospital was called and asked a series of structured questions having to do with implementation of the innovation.

One final point has to do with implementation. While hospitals were offered the possibility of receiving additional consultation visits, this in fact was never done, nor needed, until nine months of follow-up had passed.

Measurement

Four different questionnaires were used in this study. The Workshop Questionnaire was given to workshop participants at the end of the workshop. The Mail-Out Questionnaire was sent to all workshop participants three months after the workshop, with an additional mailing three weeks later to those who had not returned the first one. The Site Visitor Questionnaire was completed by all site visitors at the conclusion of their site visit. This was a brief instrument designed to assess site visitors' reactions to the site visit experience. Finally, the Telephone Follow-up Questionnaire was used as a protocol for the telephone follow-up calls at three, six, nine, and thirteen months. Both the Workshop and Mail-Out Questionnaires were similar in content and format. They both included the following principal indices of the study:

Certainty scale

This scale was designed to measure overall uncertainty about the program. It was composed of three subscales:

1. Certainty of How-To Knowledge Subscale. This subscale was composed of 10 items that had to do with the respondents' certainty of the extent to which they knew how to implement both the Small Group Ward and Lodge (α= .82);
2. Certainty of Effectiveness Subscale. This subscale was composed of five items having to do with the respondents' certainty that the Small Group Ward and Lodge were effective programs (α = .77);
3. Certainty of Feasibility Subscale. This consisted of three items having to do with the respondents' certainty that setting these programs up was feasible within the context of their hospital and community (α = .56).

The combination of the three subscale scores resulted in the score for the overall Certainty Scale, which had 18 items and a reliability of .82.

Attitude scale

The Attitude Scale was composed of eight items, dealing with the respondents' agreement with the program and its components and with their belief that the program ought to be adopted by their institution. The internal consistency reliability of this scale was .88.

Communication network item

Included on the Mail-Out Questionnaire, this item was designed to determine the extent to which each respondent had communication concerning the Lodge with each other respondent. Basically structured into a communicator X amount-of-communication matrix, data from this item were used to determine whether the Site Visit intervention increased discussion and advocacy about the program.

Degree of implementation scale

This was the principal dependent variable in the experiment and data for the measure were gathered via the Telephone Follow-up Questionnaires. The measure was essentially identical to the one described in chapter 3; the only difference being that the scale was expanded to make the highest possible score 15.75. This was done by giving a hospital one point for each Small Group Ward step, and .337 points for each Lodge step; thus, the maximum score that a hospital could receive was (7 x 1) + (26 x .337) = 15.75. The weighting was therefore identical to that used in the Degree of Implementation Scale described in chapter 3, and the two measures were psychometrically equivalent.

Additionally, a number of items dealing with demographic variables (age, time worked at hospital, etc.) and perceived participation in hospital decision making were included on the Workshop Questionnaire, as were several other minor scales which did not figure significantly in the subsequent analysis.

RESULTS

For the site visit to have its intended effect on implementation of the Lodge a particular sequence of events needed to happen: (1) the site visitor would need to be convinced that his or her hospital ought to adopt the Lodge; (2) he would then need to return home and discuss the program with his peers, acting as an advocate for the program; (3) other hospital staff would need to be convinced of the necessity and feasibility of adopting the Lodge; and (4) the necessary steps would have to be taken for adoption to occur. Given this likely order of events, we can now consider the observed effects of the Site Visit manipulation, as it relates to the hypothesized effects on discussion, perceived uncertainty, and implementation, respectively.

Effects on Discussion

To begin on an optimistic note, results of the Site Visitor Questionnaire indicated that all site visitors were convinced that their hospitals ought to adopt the program. To determine what the visitor did about this, it was necessary to examine communication and discussion patterns within the hospital. These data came primarily from a communication question on the Mail-Out Questionnaire. It was structured in a matrix format, in which each respondent indicated the amount of communication concerning the Lodge that he or she had with every other respondent. The data showed the mean strength of communication across all communication links by condition. There was no difference between conditions ($F = 2.30$; $df = 1,22$; ns). Thus, for all staff queried, discussion, as measured by this aggregated score, did not increase as a result of whatever efforts the site visitor undertook (see table 9.1).

However, a more detailed analysis revealed a somewhat different picture. An attempt was made to determine each hospital's "sociometric star," or focus of communication, defined as the person with the greatest number of incoming links from other people, on the communication question. Using empirical data from the communication network item, the individual who was nominated most in other's matrix networks was identified in each hospital. Once identified, communication patterns with that person were examined as affected by condition. The "star" received marginally stronger communication (see table 9.2) in the site visit condition than in the control condition ($F = 3.49$; $df = 1,22$; $p < .10$). This suggested, albeit weakly, that the visit probably had some kind of impact on communication within the organization, and that greater advocacy may have been taking place.

Table 9.1. Effect of Site Visit on Mean Discussion Strength.

Experimental				Control
2.80				2.67

Source	df	MS	F	p
Cond.	1	.103	2.303	ns
Hosp.	22	.045		
Total	23			

Table 9.2. Effect of Site Visit on Star's Mean Discussion.

Experimental				Control
3.56				3.18

Source	df	MS	F	p
Cond.	1	.851	3.494	$p < .1$
Hosp.	22	.244		
Total	23			

Effects on Uncertainty

What was the effect of the Site Visit on perceived uncertainty concerning effectiveness, feasibility, how-to knowledge, and evaluation of the Lodge innovation? To begin, table 9.1 shows the effect that the visit had on felt staff uncertainty concerning their "how-to" knowledge about the program. This involved questions such as "how certain are you that you know enough about the Lodge to be able to set one up?" As in the Phase I and Phase II analyses, this design is nested, hospitals within conditions. It was therefore necessary to separate out the variance due to hospitals (Winer, 1976). As is shown in table 9.3, the Site Visit had a significant effect on staff uncertainty concerning their knowledge about how to set up the program ($F = 6.25$; $df = 1,32$; p .05).

There was no significant effect for the Site Visit on staff uncertainty concerning the effectiveness of the Lodge (see table 9.4). However, there were significant differences between hospitals ($F = 1.86$; $df = 22,322$; p .05), suggesting that pre-existing organizational dynamics were exerting a residue of impact on perceived effectiveness. However, neither the site visit, nor the Hospital factor affected staff uncertainty concerning the Lodge's feasibility (see table 9.5).

Table 9.3. Effect of Site Visit on Uncertainty
of "How-to" Knowledge.

Experimental				Control
2.96				3.15

Source	df	MS	F	p
Cond.	1	2.555	6.247	$p < .05$
Hosp.	22	.454	1.110	ns
Subj.	322	.409		
Total	345			

The three previous subscales were combined and the data reanalyzed (see table 9.6). The site visit had a marginal effect on overall uncertainty ($F = 5.16$; $df = 1, 22$; $p < .10$). It can also be seen, however, that the Hospital effect is again significant and, in a sense, "smothering" the manipulation ($F = 1.60$; $df = 22, 322$; $p < .05$).

The final test of perceptual-attitudinal variables concerned the effect of the intervention on staff attitude toward the Lodge (see table 9.7). There was no significant effect.

Table 9.4.   Effect of Site Visit on Uncertainty
of Effectiveness.

Experimental   Control
    2.70   2.71

Source	df	MS	F	p
Cond.	1	.004	.006	ns
Hosp.	22	1.100	1.860	p < .05
Subj.	339	.592		
Total	362			

Table 9.5.   Effect of Site Visit on Uncertainty
of Feasibility.

Experimental   Control
    3.37   3.45

Source	df	MS	F	p
Cond.	1	.4802	1.751	ns
Hosp.	22	.3397	1.238	ns
Subj.	338	.2743		
Total	361			

Table 9.6.   Effect of Site Visit on Overall
Uncertainty.

Experimental   Control
    2.94   3.08

Source	df	MS	F	p
Cond.	1	1.238	3.230	p < .10
Hosp.	22	.383	1.597	p < .05
Subj.	303	.240		
Total	326			

Table 9.7.   Effect of Site Visit on Attitude
Toward Lodge.

Experimental				Control
3.95				3.90

Source	df	MS	F	p
Cond.	1	.157	.633	ns
Hosp.	22	.509	2.054	p < .0005
Subj.	273	.248		
Total	296			

Effects on Implementation Behaviors

It will be recalled that a hypothesis of this experiment was that the Site Visit condition would enhance the adoption and implementation of the Lodge innovation. However, inasmuch as a guiding theme of the study is the promotion of peer information exchange and network building, it was deemed desirable to look at several instrumental behaviors in addition to implementation per se. These were measured in several ways. The first way was a count of the telephone calls made to the consultant team subsequent to the site visit. These were spontaneous calls requesting some kind of information. Excluded from the count were calls concerning the scheduling of the workshop, the site visit, or any other administrative matter. The actual measure used in this case was the number of hospitals in each condition that made such calls. In other words, a hospital received a score of one (made one or more calls) or zero (made no calls) on this measure. As indicated by table 9.8, the site visit did result in more hospitals making calls to the consultants ($X^2 = 5.55$; p < .02).

The second way in which instrumental behavior was measured was by the number of hospitals that sent letters to the consultant requesting information. Table 9.7 shows that while more site visit hospitals sent letters, the difference was not significant (see table 9.8).

The final measure was related more directly to peer-to-peer instrumental behaviors. This was the number of hospitals that sent staff to visit institutions with a Lodge in addition to the original site visit host hospital in Minnesota. Table 9.8 indicates that the Site Visit condition affected visiting, although not at a statistically significant level, in that four hospitals in the Site Visit condition made visits, compared to none in the control condition. It should also be noted that, in addition to the four visits indicated in table 9.8, one site visit

Table 9.8. Effect of Site Visit on Calls,
Letters, and Visits.

| | Calls | | |
	Site Visit	Control	Total
# of hospitals that made calls	6	0	6
# of hospitals that made no calls	6	12	18
Total	12	12	

X^2 = 5.55; p <.02; df = 1

| | Letters | | |
	Site Visit	Control	Total
# of hospitals that sent letters	7	3	10
# of hospitals that sent no letters	5	9	14
Total	12	12	

X^2 = 1.54; ns; df = 1

| | Visits | | |
	Site Visit	Control	Total
# of hospitals made visits	4	0	4
# of hospitals that made no visits	8	12	20
Total	12	12	

X^2 = 2.70; ns

hospital sent personnel to visit the hospital in Minnesota on a separate occasion. Also, one of the site visitors made a visit to another site visit hospital that was beginning to implement its own Lodge. This was clearly the kind of peer-to-peer "network-building" that the Site Visit condition was intended to promote. Another point of interest is that several of the site visitors made efforts on their own to disseminate information about the Lodge to local Community Mental Health Centers, and other service agencies, while no such efforts were reported by the control hospitals.

Given the data that has been presented, it does seem that the site visit had some of the predicted process effects, specifically effects on advocacy, uncertainty, and network building.

Movement Toward Adoption

Finally, we come to the effect of the visit on actual implementation of the Lodge innovation. Adoption of the program was measured by the Degree of Implementation checklist described previously. These data were collected during the telephone follow-up calls that were made at three, six, nine and thirteen months after the workshop. Figure 9.3 shows the mean implementation score for the two conditions over time.

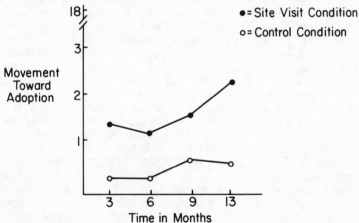

Fig. 9.3. Movement toward adoption by condition over time.

Although hospitals in the Site Visit condition evidenced a greater level of implementation at each of the four time periods, the differences only approach significance (F = 2.86; df = 1, 22; p < .11).

Table 9.9. Movement Toward Adoption by Condition.

Source	df	MS	F	p
Conditions	1	30.083	2.858	p < .11
Hospital	22	10.527		
Time	3	2.401	.767	ns
C x T	3	.801	.256	ns
H x T	66	3.129		
Total	95			

Needless to say, the consistency of the observed differences over time would raise the question as to whether a larger $\underline{N}$ would have enhanced the significance level to a more respectable figure. However, speculation aside, the data do suggest that site visits may be a useful knowledge transfer technique. More of this is discussed below.

Cluster Analysis

One additional analysis should be noted. A cluster analysis was performed with these data using the BCTRY program (Tryon and Bailey, 1970). The results of that analysis showed that the scales, scores, and items from the several questionnaires reduced to two clusters. One was a Discussion cluster, and the second could be described as a Certainty-Attitude cluster. Together they accounted for a healthy (83 percent) proportion of the variance represented by these instruments. The Certainty-Attitude cluster could be considered to represent some kind of cognitive dimension concerning the Lodge, and the Discussion cluster represented an organizational process domain. The solution was not orthogonal, and the clusters were related with a correlation of approximately .4.

As described in chapters 4 and 5, one feature of the BCTRY program is its ability to develop empirical typologies based on standardized cluster scores, or O-analysis. The results (figure 9.4) indicate that there were four organizational types based on the two clusters, as follows:

1. O-Type 1 - average Certainty and very low Discussion;
2. O-Type 2 - moderate (just above average) Certainty and moderate Discussion;

3. O-Type 3 - moderate to high Certainty and high Discussion;
4. O-Type 4 - very low Certainty and low Discussion.

In a manner analogous to procedures employed in chapters 4 and 5, an attempt was made to relate this empirical typology to hospitals' implementation of the Lodge innovation. The results of this analysis are depicted graphically in figure 9.5, and in ANOVA format in table 9.10.

As figure 9.5 shows, O-types 1 and 4, which were low on either discussion or certainty, had almost no movement toward implementation of the program; O-Type 2, which was moderate on both dimensions had some movement; and O-Type 3, which was high on both, had quite a bit of movement toward implementation. This shows that, as was suggested earlier, both certainty and discussion are related to change. Important here is the fact that not only a high level of Certainty, but also a high level of Discussion, seem to be necessary for adoption and implementation to take place. However, while they seem necessary, they are by no means sufficient to cause change. There were hospitals in both O-Types 2 and 3 that accomplished nothing in terms of adoption or implementation.

DISCUSSION

As was the case in most of the site visit studies described earlier in this chapter, the site visit intervention used in this experiment was not an overwhelming success. While the site visit does appear to have some impact on social processes within the hospital, it nevertheless had little effect on actual adoption and implementation of the Lodge innovation. In spite of these results, much can be learned about the social change process and the role that a site visit might play in it.

The site visit intervention seemed to have had some of the predicted effects on intervening process variables. It significantly affected uncertainty about how to set up the Lodge, advocacy, and instrumental behaviors related to implementation. The cluster analysis also showed that the composite variables of the Attitude-Certainty and Discussion clusters are very highly related to change. The implication therefore is that the site visit intervention is one that has impact on the correct variables, but it simply does not affect them strongly enough.

This interpretation leads to the possibility that the intervention itself ought to be expanded and intensified. This might be done by sending more staff members from the hospital on the site visit, tinkering with the organizational role of site visitors, lengthening the visit, or engaging in some kind of

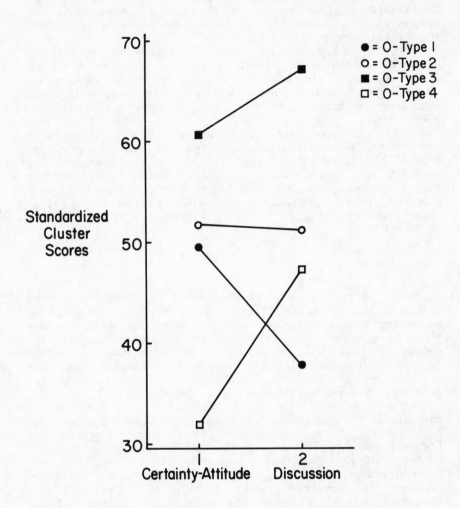

Fig. 9.4. Cluster scores of O-types.

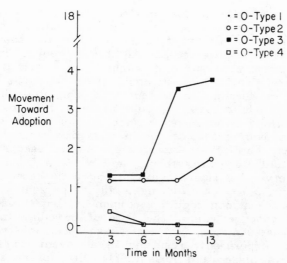

Fig. 9.5. Movement toward adoption by O-type over time.

Table 9.10.   Movement Toward Adoption by 0-Type.

Source	df	MS	F	p
0-Types	3	22.603	2.332	p < .06
Hospitals	20	9.693		
Time	3	2.401	.758	ns
T x 0	9	2.106	.665	ns
H x T	60	3.167		
Total	95			

matching process so that the organizations being visited are as similar as possible to the visitors' organizations. For example, the data of Stevens and Tornatzky (1979), and Corbett and Guttinger (1977) would argue persuasively for the expansions of the site visit to include more site visitors, at varying responsibilities in the organization. Undoubtedly, these changes might make a site visit intervention more effective, and only further experimental work can determine how much more effective such changes would make it. Certainly, there is a strong possibility that incremental improvements might, when aggregated, have considerable effect on outcome.

Another way of viewing the problem might be to consider the problem of the context in which the site visit is placed. The time at which the site visit takes place in the adoption process could be of importance, as might the order of interventions. For example, a site visit might be more effective if consultation were provided immediately after the visit took place, thereby reinforcing its content. On the other hand, the whole process might have a greater impact if the site visit were to be provided subsequent to such a consultation visit. This notion of providing consultation in close time proximity to the site visit may be of great importance. As has been shown in this book, and by Fairweather, Sanders, and Tornatzky (1974), any intervention must have a strong action component in order to have an impact on change. In the present study, the site visit had a strong cognitive component, but the action component was obscure; thus, the lack of immediate action consultation assistance may in fact have been a critical weakness of the experiment, resulting in an event similar to what happened to Glaser and Ross (1971): little or no adoption.

The O-analysis provides some additional insight into the problems of context. The analysis indicated that greater discussion and certainty were necessary, but not sufficient conditions for change. This means that there are other factors that need to be considered when designing an intervention.

It should also be noted that this represented a rather stringent test of the site visit technique. In fact, its impact might be synergistically enhanced if combined with other proven tactics. Consider the evidence provided in chapter 4 that participative decision making led to more innovation decision. It would seem a fruitful tactic to combine a site visit, which would not be expected to affect participation, with an intervention that does affect it, such as the Level of Participation intervention described in chapter 4. By the same token, the organization development intervention described in chapter 5 might be fruitfully combined with a site visit approach.

An additional factor to be considered is that of individual hospital differences. As noted in this chapter, and in the Phase I and Phase II experiments, there were significant Hospital differences on a number of variables. If it were possible to systematize these differences (Downs and Mohr, 1976), one might be able to match one's change tactics to organizational type, thereby enhancing the effectiveness of the tactics.

In conclusion, it can be said that a visit to the site of an innovative program combined with only minimal consultation assistance, is only minimally effective. What is clearly needed is further experimental research to determine if strengthening the intervention makes it more powerful, and to determine if altering the context and other kinds of assistance provided increases the effectiveness of the technique. Such research needs to be experimental in design and complex in nature in order to sort out the effects of a great diversity of variables.

10 Perils of Change Agent Training: Pilot Effort

The recurrent theme of the previous four chapters has been that peer-to-peer interaction ought to be an effective way to promote the dissemination and implementation of social innovation. However, the dismal results of the newsletter experiment, and the marginal effects of the site visit experiment on building a network, led to another rethinking of that view. Moreover, while the El Dorado experience pointed out the long-term uncertainties of relying on naturally occurring "bureaucratic entrepreneurs," it also suggested that some individuals can function as change agents, at least in their own setting. If such persons could be located, their skills and experience might be exploited in a larger national context. Perhaps if one could identify a sample of indigenous innovators, then through the provision of suitable training and incentives they could be turned into a cadre of innovation/ change consultants and "unleashed" upon the national mental health bureaucracy.

The idea of "change agent training" is not new (see Havelock, 1972), and does have a certain intuitive appeal. If one assumes that existing literature can provide a finite and manageable set of dissemination and consultation tactics, it would seem a relatively simple matter to impart these skills to a motivated group of prospective change agents. Such an opportunity emerged late in the course of this project, and what follows is a largely naturalistic description of what happened.

A PLAN FOR CHANGE AGENT TRAINING

Candidates and Recruitment

As a result of the Phase I and Phase II experiments (chap. 3-5), and of the earlier Lodge dissemination efforts (Fairweather, Sanders, and Tornatzky, 1974), as of the third year of the MSU-NIMH Innovation Diffusion Project, a fairly large number of Lodge replicates had been established across the country. Some of these programs had been operating for up to ten years; other Lodges had only recently begun. Taken in the aggregate, however, the group of people that had developed and/or were running these programs were definitionally "innovators." All of them had wended the tortuous path of innovation in their institution, and they had all mastered the numerous logistical and political hindrances to implementation. Moreover, by virtue of having established Lodge programs, these were clearly individuals who had made a personal and behavioral investment in this social innovation. Although most of these innovators had never met one another, or had rarely communicated with each other, they shared a common experience: they had all implemented the Lodge innovation in their setting, and had all helped it to survive.

These individuals then, seemed the logical foci for an effort to recruit and train a cadre of indigenous change agents. All programs listed in Lodge Notes (see chap. 7) as Lodge Innovators were called and asked to select two persons from their program staff who were interested in helping others develop the program. No attempt was made to influence these nominations. Staff selected by whatever process then received a letter from the research team inviting them to a three-day training workshop in East Lansing, Michigan. The letter introduced them to the activities of the Innovation Diffusion Project, in case they were not already familiar with them. The need for, and importance of, peer influence in Lodge diffusion was reinforced, and the intention of the workshop and their particular specific role in the process were briefly described. The more crucial sections of the recruitment letter included the following:

> We continue to be impressed with the credibility and ability of Lodge program administrators like yourself, in conveying to other staff the concepts, and nuts and bolts information, necessary to establishing a program. For example, as part of our current project we have been sending potential Lodge adopters on a "site visit" to the program at Minneapolis. This effort has been quite exciting, and also contributed to the thinking behind the meeting next month.

As you can see from the enclosed schedule, our
meeting is described as <u>Change Agent Training</u>. In
effect, we would like to build a "network" of peer-
to-peer advocacy involving attendees of the meeting.
Part of this does involve training, or perhaps more
descriptively, the imparting to you of what we have
learned in 10 years in the Lodge dissemination
business. We have gained a lot of insight in how to
approach hospitals, how to present workshops, how
to use media, and how to consult with maximum
impact. This we will give to you.

What we expect to get from you, and the other
attendees, is a plan of action, by which other
hospitals and treatment facilities can become Lodge
adopters. Obviously, your long involvement in your
own institutional battles will be a great asset in this
process. The set of activities that are outlined in
the enclosed schedule hopefully reflect the interactive nature of this "training" experience. We can
convey to you, and your peers, what we have
learned about dissemination; however, it is incum-
bent upon the group of meeting attendees, to take
this information, and based on their own experiences, reformulate it into a meaningful plan of
action.

I would invite you to respond to the schedule
of activities, and this letter, with your observations.
How can we make the meetings more meaningful?
How can we more directly build a network of change
agents?

Expenses for the workshop attendees were covered by the
project, which incidentally was a strong incentive for participating in the training experience. Representatives came
from Lodge programs in the following states: Alaska,
Arkansas, Colorado, Kansas, Michigan, Minnesota, New
Hampshire, Ohio, Oregon, Pennsylvania, Tennessee, Texas,
and Wisconsin. In all, 34 individuals eventually attended the
training session. Some programs sent more than two people,
at their own expense.

The Training Experience

Quite obviously, the training effort could not merely be
comprised of a highly structured transmission of facts, skills,
and consultation tactics. The workshop was to be much more

than "educational" in the strict sense of that term. The research team hoped to accomplish three objectives in the training-workshop experience: (1) to convince these innovators that they ought to become "change agents" beyond their immediate setting and to become actively involved in national dissemination and consultation activities; (2) to convey professional and technical skills concerning making presentations, consulting, approaching organizations, and the like; (3) to create a sense of esprit de corps among the attendees such that a true "network" of innovators could and would eventually emerge; and (4) to articulate how the research team would provide logistical and financial support for the effort.

To approach accomplishment of these objectives within three days time called for an intensive and variegated training format. What emerged was a plan that would include formal presentation of materials, juxtaposed with attendee discussion and reaction to those materials. In addition, considerable opportunity was provided for unstructured "social" interaction. The schedule of training is depicted in figure 10.1.

For example, the three-day meeting began with an introduction to the need for training disseminators and for network building. Participants were then allocated two hours for introducing themselves to one another, sharing their program accomplishments, and in describing recurrent problems in their setting. This session was "show and tell" writ large.

The research staff then presented their work on dissemination by sharing techniques and problems encountered in: (1) approaching a hospital; (2) presenting a workshop; and (3) conducting consultations. In these presentations, handouts illustrating step-by-step activities in dissemination were distributed. Workbooks were printed to accompany each of the three presentations. Sample workshop speeches about the Lodge, examples of letters of introduction about the program, and consultation troubleshooting forms were contained in the workbooks. Each of these presentations by research staff was matched with time allocated to attendee discussion of the content, and to the development of plans to incorporate it into their own subsequent change agent activities.

The intention was to make the dissemination activity as simple and palatable as possible for the trainees. It was felt that the attendees had neither the time nor the resources to prepare elaborate training and consultation materials. By example, a slide-tape package, brochures, and manuals accompanied the various workbooks. These materials were to be used at the participant's discretion and were packaged as a training unit for their use within their institution and in their dissemination and consultation efforts. Research staff briefly demonstrated how the materials could be used and the participants critiqued the newly created slide-tape show.

Day I

Morning Session
8:30-12:00   Goals of the Conference
                     Project staff outline goals
                     Introduction of Adopters-
                     Participants introduce themselves and describe their program

Afternoon Session
1:30-3:00   Problems of Approaching and Entering
                 Hospitals
                     1. Project staff present their experience and techniques.
                     2. Participants develop plans about approaching and gaining entry.
3:15-5:30   Workshops and Presentations
                     1. Project staff presents workshop materials and techniques used and
                         present the slide-tape show developed for adopters use.
                     2. Participants evaluate the slide-tape show and develop workshop plans.

Day II

Morning Session
8:30-12:00   Consultation
                     1. Project staff present types of assistances given in consultation ses-
                         sions and share the use of organizational development technique.
                     2. Participants develop consultation plans and report them to staff for
                         feedback.

Afternoon Session
1:30-5:00   Internal Communication
                     1. MSU staff will discuss several alternatives for increasing the degree
                         of communication between members of the group of Lodge adopters.
                         Discussion will be directed toward the concept of group input to, or
                         take over of, the Lodge Notes newsletter, possible attendance at
                         conferences, forming of professional associations, and whatever
                         suggestions that can be developed from the group itself.
                     2. After the group devises a plan, they will present it to the staff for
                         feedback and discussion.

Day III

Morning Session
8:30-12:00   Final Logistics

The entire morning will be devoted to a free-ranging discussion about issues left unresolved.
This will include how to admit new adopting hospitals to the dissemination group, what their
territories would be, and how future monies will be expended. Considerable discussion will also
be directed to all as to how to insure the permanence of the dissemination group, how communication between them as a group will be handled, how liaison with the MSU staff will be
arranged, etc. The final task performed by the group will be the assignment of target
hospitals among the group members. As in all the previous tasks, the assignments will be a
mutual decision among all members of the group.

Fig. 10.1.   Change Agent Training – A meeting of lodge
             disseminators and adopters.

The afternoon of the second day and the third day's morning session were devoted to specific network-building and dissemination issues. The general purpose of these sessions was to promote further "groupness" in the form of collective decision making, planning, and the like.

The workshop as it unfolded

Bringing people who have a variety of individual goals together to work as a group is an arduous task. Although the expectations for the workshop were explicitly stated in the letters of invitation, and in the schedule, it became clear that not all the attendees shared our worldview. In fact, attendees differed widely with the project staff's planned structure of the workshop, and modifications to the original plan became inevitable.

In the unstructured sharing of problems on the first day, it became clear that two types of attendees were represented: the "old-timers" and the "fledglings." The fledglings felt an overpowering need to learn how to maintain their programs, and this need superceded all other issues - such as diffusing the program. These participants wanted to share problems that they were experiencing, and to learn solutions to those problems. These needs created a powerful interaction pattern between staff from the older and newer programs. The staff from the new programs were looking toward the more established Lodge programs - the oldtimers - for answers to their problems. In turn, the oldtimers were flattered by the attention and questioning.

The desire to exchange information among themselves about their programs immediately affected the tone of the first day's meeting. Some of the participants felt that the discussion of dissemination was introduced too early in the schedule. Some time was spent discussing whether the format should be discarded, but eventually the agenda was followed largely as planned.

At the close of the first day's meeting, a few participants continued to express general feelings of dissatisfaction because the meetings were not providing sufficient time for the members to talk among themselves, or to learn more about each others' programs and experiences; as verbalized by one attendee, "Before the group can be helpful to others, it must be helpful to each other as a group." Recognizing these needs, the presentations beginning the morning of the second day were given in a more discursive and participative style. More opportunities were allowed for participants to tell "war stories" about their own setting. Using these real anecdotes, the group came to grapple with how it could hypothetically help other programs during implementation.

Laying the groundwork for the network

Over the course of the workshop, an idea began to emerge among the participants that a more permanent vehicle for interaction and mutual support would be desirable. Since the afternoon session of the second day, and the third day were devoted to answering the question, "where do we go from here?," the group used the time to address network development of a more substantive nature. Three topics were salient: (1) setting up a nonprofit organization to continue the program; (2) identifying attendees willing to discuss and share the Lodge program with other interested people; and (3) discussing the future of Lodge Notes and other media information necessary for the future visibility and survival of the Lodge innovation.

After much discussion, the group decided that an ongoing formal organization was needed. It was mutually agreed that work be initiated on creating a nonprofit organization, and that by-laws and goals of the organization should be drawn up and circulated to all attendees. The preliminary goals which the group identified for the organization were: (1) advocacy for ex-patients; (2) teaching Lodge programs to others; (3) forming a support system for each other; and (4) meeting the needs of the chronic mentally ill population.

In discussion about the organization of the proposed nonprofit corporation, it was decided that board members should be selected by geographic regions. States were assigned to regions, and it was decided that two regional representatives would be selected for each of the four regions. These representatives became the interim members of the first board to establish the nonprofit corporation and to formulate the by-laws, working in conjunction with the research staff.

Logistics for dissemination

In addition to the above mentioned network building activities, the research staff also attempted to structure the groups future change agent and dissemination activities. Prior to the training workshop, a "hot prospects" list of names of staff at other hosppitals who had indicated an interest in implementing the Lodge had been assembled. This had been accomplished as part of the Lodge Notes experiment described in chapter 7. These were distributed to the workshop attendees on the last day, and dissemination "territories" divided up.

Considerable effort was devoted to outlining the support role to be played by the research staff in subsequent dissemination efforts by attendees. Several thousands of dollars of the grant budget had been set aside to cover the future travel costs of this cadre of ostensible change agents. The arrangements were that any of the workshop attendees could

contact a hot prospect anywhere in the country, gain agreement for a workshop presentation or consultation, and the
research project would pick up travel expenses. In addition,
the research team agreed to provide letters of introduction,
background materials on prospective hospitals, or any other
support materials that might be needed. This was in addition
to the manuals and slide-tape modules previously described.
Every conference attendee left with a large cardboard box
filled with goodies - manuals, tapes, brochures, sample
letters, etc. They also left with an unequivocal commitment on
the part of the research team to support them organizationally,
financially, and logistically.

Post Conference Events

The immediate post mortem

Whether we had in fact created a cadre of dissemination/
implementation change agents remained to be seen. As part of
a post-conference evaluation exercise, participants were asked
to evaluate the training experience on a brief questionnaire.
The resulting data were generally positive, but disturbingly
ambivalent in many specifics.

In response to an open-ended question asking their
opinion of what was accomplished in the three-day training
session, the majority indicated that the main accomplishment
was the creation of the network. A few people indicated that
the major accomplishment was the formation of a team effort
toward dissemination, and advocacy, of the Community Lodge
program, but this was a minor theme. Others identified the
formation of the board and the tentative plans for a corporate
structure as important.

When asked what they envisioned as their role in any
network or structure that might evolve, responses ranged from
uncertain to a list of contingencies. One person said, "it's
unclear"; another said, "it depends on what support MSU can
provide." One individual specifically said that he would be
"available to consult if the money was provided and if the
agency gave him time to do this." The degree of ambivalence
about assuming the role of change agent was noteworthy and is
evidenced in this quote: "At this point, I need the system-
network for my own development, and I'm not at the point of
being able to 'diffuse' much of anything."

When asked what they did expect the network to accomplish in the following year, many people indicated that they
primarily wanted to see support of existing Lodges, and the
establishment of a formal association to continue the communication exchange among Lodge adopters. Although there
was some reference to dissemination of the Lodge program to
others, the primary goals were maintaining existing programs,

promoting exchange of information, and solidifying the proposed organization for the network. A handful of people
expressed hope of establishing new Lodges and of promoting
knowledge of the Lodge to others. Finally, a few respondents
were quite skeptical about what the network might accomplish,
and expected very little to happen in the forseeable future.
The acute vision of this latter group will be demonstrated
below.

Interim support activities

Despite the mixed flavor of the above reactions, the research
team felt sufficiently positive - and logistically commited - to
continue to facilitate network-building and dissemination
activities. After the training session, a series of corres-
pondences was initiated by research staff to the conference
attendees. The first correspondence involved mailing the
minutes of the training session and a summary of decisions
that were made at the meeting. Accompanying the minutes was
a directory of addresses and phone numbers of the interim
board members, and of all participants in the training session.
    In a second mailing some weeks later, the research staff
sent participants a tentative proposal for the corporation's
by-laws and articles of incorporation for their review and
comment. Participants were also asked to suggest a name for
the corporation, and to consider what the membership dues
should be. After several weeks of no response from the
participants, the regional interim board members were called
for their assistance in prodding participants, and not even all
interim board members responded to the request, despite the
fact that these board members were ostensibly the sociometric
choices of the emerging group. In essence, very little action
was taken in response to the proposed by-laws and articles of
incorporation.
    A third letter was sent, reiterating logistical and
strategic information about dissemination activities. This was
sent to all participants who had expressed the slightest
interest in diffusing the program to other hospitals. The list
of "hot prospects" was again distributed, and the procedures
for travel reimbursement repeated. Additional suggestions for
approaching the "hot prospects" were also included, as were
brief sketches of the "hot prospect" hospitals. These capsule
sketches were drawn from nonconfidential data derived from
the Phase I study (chapter 4), and from the previous Lodge
dissemination experiment (Fairweather, Sanders and Tornatzky,
1974). Information included prior level of commitment, degree
of interest in the Lodge program, and the name of the
superintendent at the time of previous communication with the
project. In addition, the address and phone number of the
organization were attached to the description.

Needless to say, these "support activities" on the part of the research staff were both laborious and time-consuming. Neverthless, we still assumed that these stimuli were producing some reactions on the part of network members. It appears in retrospect, however, that we were playing to an empty auditorium.

THE NON-WORKING NETWORK

During the four months following the Change Agent Training Meeting, only one person used the Innovation Diffusion Project travel expenses to diffuse the program. Several of the Lodges had accommodated site visitors who had come to review their program, but no overt attempt was made by workshop attendees to travel, to provide onsite consultations, and to give workshops about the Lodge program, or to contact the "hot prospect" hospitals. Passivity was the rule, not the exception. Given the lack of action taken in the diffusion of the Lodge, the research staff decided to survey participants about why they did not participate in this ostensibly inactive activity.

Method and Procedures

The diffusion-network survey

A questionnaire was contructed to assess the innovators' felt need for a network, their perception of their roles in the network, their role in diffusion, and their behaviors supporting diffusion activities. The survey contained both open-ended questions, and forced choice items.

Procedures

Questionnaires were mailed to all workshop participants four months after the training meeting. Of the 34 surveys mailed, 33 were returned. A rough content analysis was performed on the open-ended items, and nominal choice items aggregated accordingly.

Results

Overall assessment

When asked about continuing commitment, the respondents were generally still quite interested in future participation in the

network structure.   When presented with various options, only
3 out of 32 expressed "no interest."   The range of responses
is portrayed in figure 10.2.

                    12 Active members
                     9 Regional Representatives
                     8 Interested, but inactive members
                     3 Not Interested

Fig. 10.2. Future role in network.

    In fact, when asked for suggestions for improving the
network, two-thirds of the respondents did not propose any
changes at all.   The suggestions that were indicated were
primarily positive in tone, and minor in nature.

Interest in and impediments to change agentry

Another question dealt specifically with the role that respondents foresaw for themselves regarding future dissemination/
consultation activities.   Surprisingly, two-thirds of the
adopters are still willing to do some consulting with other
interested staff, and more than half were willing to travel
away from their locale to consult.   Figure 10.3 describes their
choices.   There were no significant differences between old
and new adopters on their willingness to diffuse.

    17   Willing to travel and to consult with interested
         staff that want to start Lodge.
     6   Willing only to consult by phone and to en-
         courage them to visit my program.
     8   Interested, but not willing to commit myself at
         this time.
     1   Not interested in this sort of activity.

Fig. 10.3. Role in diffusion of lodges.

    Although the majority of respondents indicated a verbal
willingness to consult and to diffuse the innovation actively,
these data are somewhat suspect.   Given the precipitant for
deployment of the survey (no dissemination behavior) the
research team felt compelled to examine the impediments to
consultation and diffusion activities with some scrutiny.
Content analysis of the item, "What impediments, if any,
prevent you from being actively involved in consultation and
diffusion activities?," yielded a variety of responses.   Clearly

the diffusion role is not one that is readily incorporated into our Lodge adopters existing work role. The most frequent impediment identified was that of being <u>overextended</u>. Other factors mentioned in order of frequency were: (1) not acceptable part of the job description; (2) wanting reimbursement for consulting; (3) no time allocated to travel; and (4) pressing job-related variables.

That fulltime job priorities supercede the role of change agent is clear from these responses. Local job responsibilities do not readily lend themselves to engaging in extracurricular diffusion activities, especially when this would involve travel. It appears overwhelmingly that issues and responsibilities close to home prevented our trainees from "moonlighting" as change agents. While discouraging perhaps, this finding has important policy implications. When asked what the research group could do to reduce these impediments, two-thirds of the respondents had no suggestions, and the remainder wanted the research team to facilitate diffusion activities by prodding them to take action, and to increase the incentives for such activity.

Diffusion action taken

Information was also gathered on the amount of change agent behavior that had occurred during the four month period. When asked whether they had personally contacted hospitals on the "hot prospects" list, only five persons indicated that they had initiated contact. One person corresponded by letter; two persons made phone calls, and two visited other programs. Sixteen persons, however, indicated that they had received site visitors or had made consultation trips, by request, to programs not on the "hot prospect" list. More than half of the respondents had received requests for information concerning the innovation. Receiving site visitors on an informal basis seemed to be a very popular procedure with our sample, but it was almost never followed up with consultation visits to the site visitor locale. Once again, there is a strong disinclination to leave the home turf unportected, and to intrude into other organizations. None of the respondents was involved in what could be described as a consultation relationship with another institution.

Rank ordering innovation, maintenance, diffusion and association priorities

To gain a perspective of the respondents relative concern for their own Lodge program's diffusion activities, an item was included in the questionnaire that attempted to force choices among these options. Each person was asked to rank order their priorities from one to seven, high to low.

Inspection of the ranks for each of the seven activities yielded three clusters of activities rather than seven discrete choices. Kendall's concordance coefficient was .88 for the rank ordering of the three groupings. Clearly the highest priority was ensuring the immediate survival of their own program. Second priority included activities within their local community, such as expanding the present program, starting new programs in their community, and persuading local leaders to support community based interventions. The lowest priority was attached to activities dealing with promoting Lodge programs across the country, participating actively in a national association of Lodge adopters, and lobbying for Lodges. These priorities obviously reflect the respondents' concern for first attending to their home base operation and their immediate community and lastly engaging in national activities. One respondent best captures the priorities by the statement, "the smoother things are going on the home front, the easier it is to set priorities on expanding the program."

In brief, the adopters may have indicated a well-meaning willingness to participate in the network and to diffuse the innovation when such role behaviors are presented in the abstract, but when asked to rank those new roles relative to their current job description, and to the responsibilities of running their own program, the network and diffusion roles assume considerably less importance. The rank-ordered priorities more accurately reflected the lack of participation in the network and in diffusion activities.

Summary and Implications

The summary finding from this pilot effort is that an obviously motivated group of innovators, even when provided with training and resources, are not likely to become either active or effective change agents to other settings. The principal impediment to engaging in dissemination/consultation activity seems to be the pressures and demands of maintaining their own innovative program. The issues of routinization discussed in chapter 8 are also operative here. At bottom, the vision of low-cost parttime change agents seems ill-considered. While willing to show their programs to site visitors and the curious, they are not willing to reach out and generate interest and awareness of the innovation.

It might be useful, however, for analytic purposes, to contrast our experience - largely a failure - with other more successful deployments of local, indigenous innovators as change agents. The most obvious example is found in the National Diffusion Network (Emrick, 1977) in education. Here there has been a rather successful use as change consultants of persons who have developed, and currently run innovative programs. The crucial differences appear to lie in the degree of legitimization, visibility, and support afforded the local innovator. In the NDN, the program innovator is provided with considerable resources to support both the program and dissemination, is officially and prominently ushered into the network, and is the recipient of considerable symbolic and tangible incentives. Rather than being a threat to continued program survival, participation in the National Dissemination Network has positive survival value.

For numerous reasons, our effort to promote indigenous change agentry was lower-keyed, less visible, and resource-poor. It was not enough. By extension, the experience described in this chapter would argue for a more permanent, legitimated role for local innovators in dissemination networks - one not likely to be achieved by mere persuasion, goodwill, and a travel account.

11 An Overview

In any summative review of a research project of this magnitude, it is essential that one capture both the significant detailed findings, and their broad gauge implications for policy makers. We will attempt to retain that mixture of the specific and the general in this chapter. We believe that the results of this study ought to be of interest both to the scholarly community involved in innovation process research, and to federal, state, and local officials charged with promoting innovation.

It would also perhaps be useful to review the underlying rationale for the project, and for the various studies undertaken. If a "generic hypothesis" could be articulated for the book, it might be that change and innovation without human contact and interpersonal interaction, are not likely to be either benefical or complete. Conversely, if change agents and dissemination programs can facilitate a greater magnitude of interaction and discussion in organizations involved in innovation, then, perhaps, there will be a higher probability of the innovation process proceeding to a successful conclusion.

Chapters 3, 4, and 5 described a set of experiments in which project staff attempted to foster a higher degree of participative decision making and a more robust version of group problem solving and task accomplishment than is the norm in our sample of public service bureaucracies. The Phase I experiment (a 3X2X2 factorial) focused on various manipulations and interventions designed to alter organizational processes and structures relative to decision making. The Phase II experiment involved a direct test of Organization Development Techniques in fostering innovation adoption and implementation.

Chapters 6 through 10 represent a set of relatively independent studies united by the common theme of concern with peer-to-peer innovation networks. In effect, these studies explored the feasibility of decentralized, peer-dominated dissemination-of-innovation networks, as opposed to the usual centrally directed dissemination efforts (such as embodied to a limited degree by our own Michigan-based project team). How to promote the spread of innovation practices by peer-to-peer interaction - if that is indeed possible - was our concern. What then did we find out in these two sets of studies?

THE FINDINGS

In the following presentation of results we will attempt to retain the conceptual distinction between data from the Phase I and Phase II experiments, and findings from the studies of peer interaction phenomena and innovation. Although obviously related, it seems useful from a conceptual, as well as a policy, point of view to keep the two sets of studies distinct.

THE PHASE I AND PHASE II EXPERIMENTS

Facilitating Participative Decision Making

The complex Phase I experimental manipulations had a relatively simple common purpose: to promote through brief alterations in organizational structures and processes a wider and more intense involvement in decision making relative to a social innovation. The hypothesis was that such changes would increase the likelihood that a decision to adopt would occur.

One very general - and important - finding of the Phase I experiment was that it was operationally possible to bring off the manipulations. It should be noted that the experimental variables studied here are normally not considered "policy levers" since many assume that they are not manipulable at all. Prior to the study, there was considerable skepticism as to whether the necessary brevity of our intervention would permit us to produce any real, and perceived, changes in participativeness. Fortunately, it would and we did. Across several of the measures and conditions there were significant effects of felt involvement in decision making. Interestingly, the effects on perceived and felt participativeness (as measured by questionnaire responses) was considerably more apparent in those conditions which focused on process (Group Enhancement) as opposed to structural manipulations (such as the number and role of decisionmaking participants).

A related and even more counter-intuitive set of findings were those relating the intervening variable of participation to the dependent variable of adoption decisions. Across the three experimental conditions, and considering the respective adoption decisions of volunteering for a workshop and volunteering for consultation, only the experimental condition that manipulated the role of participants in decision making had a statistically significant effect on adoption decisions. This is relatively unambiguous support for the utility of involving line personnel, as opposed to exclusively administrators, in innovation decisions.

Finally, a set of exploratory findings shed light on the usefulness of the concept of organizational type; as Downs and Mohr (1976) have pointed out, the "secondary characteristics" or organization-innovation interactions may have considerable explanatory power in understanding innovation processes. We found that organization typologizing on intraorganizational dimensions can indeed discriminate innovativeness, and that organizational features may have considerable longitudinal stability. Organizational type may have more predictive utility than the usual univariate organizational descriptors such as state-federal affiliation, size, and the like. This area clearly needs further research.

Enhancing Organizational Capacity

While the Phase II experiment was, in effect, a "test" of Organizational Development techniques, the nature of that test was a significant departure from the prevailing ideology and perspective of OD practice. Rather than using Organizational Development as the primary focus of a change intervention, OD was employed in the experimental condition as an adjunct to a highly directive, task-oriented set of consultations designed to promote a specific innovation. The assumption behind the experiment was that since the process of implementation puts so many demands on the implementing organization, that process might be enhanced if attention were focused on building organizational capacity for change.

The results of the Phase II experiment were in the predicted direction. The OD intervention did have a significant impact on the cohesiveness and interaction patterns of the group of Lodge implementers. Moreover, those effects on group process translated into a significantly greater movement over time toward full implementation of the innovation in those settings in which Organizational Development was deployed. In short, this experimental wedding of OD to a directive dissemination effort was a success.

Other findings of Phase II reinforced the importance of group process, as witnessed by several correlational relationships. In addition, further attempts were made to create a predictive typologizing of organizations from the sample in a manner analoguous to analyses in the Phase I experiment. The potential utility for pursuing this kind of research was again demonstrated.

Summary of Phase I and Phase II

Taken together the results of these experiments tend to support the generic hypotheses of the study: change agent activities that can promote interaction and build the group processes of the adopting group will have a facilitating effect on the innovation process. Although the manipulations attempted in these two experiments were not uniformly successful in that regard, the findings do suggest the usefulness of further research in this area. Incremental gains in innovation adoption and implementation can be obtained by a focus on intraorganizational variables. Moreover, these studies are testimony to the fact that consultation, and "change agentry," need not be considered black arts; they can be subjected to scientific scrutiny, and in fact to experimentation. This is a circumstance that many OD practitioners would be loath to acknowledge, as would many "decision makers." The policy implications of this fact, and of the findings themselves, will be considered below.

PEER PROCESSES AND INNOVATION

Chapters 6 through 10 represented various attempts to understand, perchance to experiment with, situations in which indigenous peer relations assume a central importance in the diffusion of innovation. This was in contrast to the typical centralized, well-orchestrated dissemination network usually established by professional change agents. There were several reasons - both from conceptual and public policy concerns - for examining these issues. Conceptually, the study of peer-dominated dissemination networks represents a natural extension of the general notion of participation and social interaction that have been the central focus of this book. For reasons discussed in chapters 6 through 10, peer-to-peer dissemination activities may empirically be a very powerful approach to overcome many of the inhibiting forces involved in the innovation process. By the same token, recent years have witnessed a groundswell of cynicism about centralized government activity, including centrally directed dissemination, training, and assistance programs (e.g., Schon, 1971). The facilitation of decentralized peer-dominated networks - or the feasibility thereof - would seem to be a meaningful research area.

A Baseline Study

The first research question considered in this series of studies was the extent to which a peer-to-peer innovation network already existed among our sample of psychiatric hospitals. Based on questionnaire responses to a query about programmatic information exchange, an interorganizational network analysis was performed. As reported in chapter 6, the results were relatively clear cut. Based on our data, we found no evidence of a peer network that transcended fairly limited regional or bureaucratic boundaries. The networks found among state hospitals in the sample tended to be quite "provincial" and restricted to contiguous geography; networks found among the Veterans Administration hospitals in the sample did not extend beyond the federal system itself.

These findings suggest that if a peer-dominated innovation network is deemed a meaningful public policy goal, it is not likely to blossom spontaneously. Clearly, some amount of assistance, encouragement, or support will be necessary to ensure its establishment.

A Low Profile Intervention

Given that a national peer network was not obviously present in our sample, the first intervention study was an attempt to prod the facilitation of network activities gently. As described in chapter 7, a national newsletter was developed, and employed in a treatment/no treatment experimental design, The overall intention of the newsletter was to promote interaction, visiting, and mutual help between prior adopters of the Lodge innovation (who were spotlighted in the newsletter) and their peers across the country (who were the principal recipients of the newsletter).

Without elaborating on the dismal, the results of this experiment were crystal clear. This type of low profile, minimally intrusive intervention was of no use whatsoever in promoting network activity, at least among this sample of organizations. The significance of this nonsignificant finding will be considered elsewhere.

The El Dorado Experience

The effect of the El Dorado case study was to reinforce the research team's hypotheses about the viability of peer-dominated innovation processes. As a serendipitous extension of the project activities dealing with peer networks, an opportunity presented itself for real-time observation of a relatively successful peer network. Situated in a large western state, the "bureaucratic entrepreneurs" (Lambright, 1977) in this drama were two central office staff members. Working in collaboration with members of the research team, they were able to provide the impetus for the eventual implementation of several replicates of the Lodge innovation. In short, the case study provided evidence that indigenous change agents, properly situated and motivated, can promote innovation in their own system.

There were, however, several findings in the case study that qualify the general positive nature of the evidence. It was very clear that the implementations in El Dorado were relatively fragile. Few if any of the Lodge replicates had achieved the degree of routinization that might predict extended longevity. The implication is that while a small group of indigenous change agents may achieve the implementation of innovation practices, in the absence of explicit legitimization and support, the net effect of their efforts may be nil. This too has policy implications that will be discussed below.

Site Visiting

The site visit experiment discussed in chapter 9 was an attempt to exploit some of the benefits of indigenous change agent activity (witnessed in the El Dorado experience) in the context of a more structured collaboration with research staff. The experimental intervention in this study supplemented a standard workshop training experience with a site visit, for selected hospital staff, to an exemplary Lodge program. The control condition provided no site visit opportunity.

The results of the experiment were mixed. While the site visit tended to reduce felt uncertainties about the innovation, it had only a marginal effect on actual implementation. Once again, although peer-dominated dissemination activities had a slight effect in the predicted direction, the tenuousness of that effect was obvious.

Training Indigenous Change Agents

Finally, chapter 10 described an effort to promote a peer-dominated dissemination network by the training of prior

adopters of the innovation in consultation techniques and
change tactics. In addition, resources and logistical support
were provided. The results were also among the most clear of
any of the peer process studies. Little impact was found as a
result of the training, network-building intervention. The
encouragement, and logistical support, necessary for mobilizing
a peer-dominated dissemination network were beyond the
intervention attempted here.

Summary of the Peer Process Studies

Taken together, the studies reported in chapters 6 through 10
do not provide overwhelming support for the concept of
peer-dominated dissemination networks, at least not as operationalized here. The results at the same time highlighted
some of the promise of peer networks, as well as exposing the
weaknesses. Indigenous peer networks can facilitate innovation processes, as illustrated in the El Dorado experience,
and to a lesser degree by the site visit experiment, but such
networks do not appear to occur spontaneously with great
frequency, and moreover seem distinctly difficult to create.
The relatively low level interventions of media promotion and
the training of change agents that we tried as network
building were fairly ineffective. In summary, if peer processes are deemed desirable component of dissemination
networks, considerably more effort, resources, and legitimation
needs to be devoted to their nurturing.

POLICY IMPLICATIONS

In chapter 1, we attempted to build a strong case for the
necessity to reform American public service bureaucratics, and
a parallel argument for the deployment of innovative practices
and technologies in order to accomplish that goal. What has
been learned as a result of these studies to contribute to that
discussion?
      It should be noted that these are concerns of national
policy significance. The federal sector is heavily invested in
programs to transfer technological innovation (see Executive
Office of the President, 1977) across various sectors. These
range from the well-worn agricultural extension system to more
recent initiatives in education, housing, mental health, and the
like. Across these various programs there is wide variance in
the extent to which formal media as opposed to process-
intensive dissemination is employed, the degree of central-
ization versus indigenous-local involvement, and the extent to
which technology transfer efforts are informed by empirical

data. As a result of the studies reported here, several
recommendations and suggestions may be made.

One obvious conclusion from this study, and from the
previous mental health dissemination effort of Fairweather,
Sanders, and Tornatzky (1974), is that the promotion of a
complex social innovation is indeed difficult. After more than
eight years of effort and two national studies, the number of
Lodge replicates actually implemented is small relative to the
population of hospitals. One could, of course, argue that the
nature of the Lodge innovation - or of the researchers themselves - was so repugnant that the generalizability of these
findings is questionable, but a more likely conclusion would be
that all complex innovations - ones that demand extensive
organizational dislocations - will be difficult to implement. The
policy implication is that in order to transfer such technologies
and practices, an intensive, organizational process-oriented
approach to dissemination may be essential.

Moreover, the significant findings from the Phase I and
Phase II experiments in this book would suggest that organizational process can be easily manipulated in the context of
a national dissemination effort. More importantly, such
interventions can enhance the likelihood of implementation.
Admittedly, the significant enhancing effects found in this
study (the staff/administrators manipulation in Phase I; the OD
intervention in Phase II) were not of an extraordinary magnitude. However, these interventions are replicable, and
could be built into dissemination programs. Furthermore,
there are directions for subsequent research suggested by the
findings. It is possible to foresee the development of a set of
operational procedures to be incorporated into dissemination/
technology transfer programs as a result of extending this
body of research.

The findings on peer dissemination networks also have
policy relevance. That such networks do not seem too
prominent, and seem difficult to facilitate with the minimal
interactions attempted here, argue for greater efforts and
resources devoted to intensive dissemination activity. The
findings on the neglible utility of printed media in fostering
innovation processes replicates an old theme (e.g., Fairweather, Sanders and Tornatzky, 1974): that impersonal
communication is a relatively useless dissemination technique.

In a very general sense, the study strongly suggests
that much more needs to be done to link programmatic R&D to
institutional practice. The prevailing assumption among
mission agencies involved in applied research is that eventually
the results will "trickle down," and improve practices in the
field. Our intensive efforts over the past ten years to
promote that link have only barely increased the implementation
prospects of a single innovation. When we juxtapose that
experience with the vast need for improved services in public

agencies, this plea for "more" may seem reasonable. When compared with the resources, time, and manpower devoted to technological change and dissemination in an area like agriculture, it is no wonder that so little meaningful change has occurred in areas like mental health.

One final recommendation (though it may appear self-serving) should be made to policy makers. Empirically, we still know very little about how change and innovation occur in complex organizations. More - and more targeted - research to consolidate existing findings is needed. Although we are far from having created a "technology" of innovation processes, the closer we come to that goal, the better for the American consumer of public services.

Bibliography

Argyris, C. Interpersonal competence and organizational effectiveness. Homewood, Ill.: The Dorsey Press, 1972.

Avellar, J. W., Dittmar, S.J., Tornatzky, L. G., Fergus, E. O., Fleischer, M., and Fairweather, G. W. The community lodge program. East Lansing, Mich.: Michigan State University, 1978.

Aylen, D., Anderson, D., and Wideen, M. "Situations and characteristics related to the adoption and implementation of innovative practices." Educational Research Institute of British Columbia, Canada, 1977.

Behr, G. Research-based considerations for effective program implementation. Paper presented at the meeting of the American Educational Research Association, March, 1978.

Bennett, E. B. Discussion, decision, commitment, and consensus in group decision. Human Relations, 29 (1955): 251-274.

Berman, P., and McLaughlin, M. W. Federal programs supporting educational change, vol. IV: The findings in review. Santa Monica, Calif.: Rand Corp., 1978.

Berne, E. Games people play. New York: Grove Press, 1964.

Berscheid, E. Opinion change and communicator-communicatee similarity. Journal of Personality and Social Psychology, 4 (1966): 670-680.

Bond, M. H., and Tornatzky, L. G. Locus of control in students from Japan and the United States: Dimensions and levels of response. Psychologia, 16 (1973): 28-32.

Boruch, R. Bibliography: Randomized field experiments for planning and evaluating social programs. Evaluation, 2 (1974): 83-87.

Boruch, R. F., and Gomez, H. Sensitivity, bias, and theory in impact evaluation. Professional Psychology, 8, no. 4 (1977): 411-433.

Bowers, D. G., and Seashore, S. E. Changing the structure and functioning of an organization. In W. M. Evan (ed.), Organizational experiments: Laboratory and field research. New York: Harper & Row, 1971.

Brock, T. C. Communicator-recipient similarity and decision change. Journal of Personality and Social Psychology, 1 (1965): 650-654.

Burns, T., and Stalker, G. The management of innovation. London: Tavistock Publications, 1961.

Calsyn, R. J., Tornatzky, L. G., and Dittmar, S. Incomplete adoption of an innovation: The case of goal attainment scaling. Evaluation, 4 (1977): 127-130.

Campbell, D. T., and Stanley, J. C. Experimental and quasi-experimental designs for research. Chicago: Rand McNally, 1963.

Caplan, N. A minimal set of conditions necessary for the utilization of social science knowledge in policy formulation at the national level. In C. H. Weiss (ed.), Using social research in public policy making. Lexington, Mass.: Lexington Books, 1977.

Chalupsky, A. G., and Coles, G. J. The unfulfilled promise of educational innovation. Paper presented at the meeting of the American Educational Research Association, New York, 1977.

Chu, F. D., and Trotter, S. The madness establishment. New York: Grossman, 1974.

Clausen, J. A., Seidenfeld, M. A., and Deasy, L. O. Parent attitudes toward participation of their children in polio vaccine trials. American Journal of Public Health, 44 (1954): 1526-1536.

Coch, K., and French, J. R. P., Jr. Overcoming resistance to change. Human Relations, 1 (1948): 512-532.

Coleman, J., Katz, E., and Menzel, H. The diffusion of an Innovation among physicians. Sociometry, 20 (1957): 253-270.

Corbett, W. T., and Guttinger, H. I. The assumptions, strategies, and results of a linkage model for dissemination. Paper presented at the meeting of the American Educational Research Association, New York, April 1977.

Cox, D. R. Planning of experiments. New York: John Wiley
    & Sons, Inc., 1958.

Davis, H. Four ways to goal attainment. Evaluation, 1
    (1973): 43-48.

Downs, A. Inside bureaucracy. Boston: Little, Brown,
    1967.

Downs, G. W., and Mohr, L. B. Conceptual issues in the
    study of innovation. Administrative Science Quarterly, 21
    (1976): 200-214.

Emrick, J. A. Evaluation of the national diffusion network.
    Vol. 1: Findings and recommendations. Final report to
    the U.S. Office of Education. Menlo Park, Calif.: Stan-
    ford Research Institute, May 1977.

Eveland, J. D., Rogers, E. M., and Klepper, C. The inno-
    vative process in public organizations. Some elements of
    a preliminary model. Springfield, Va.: National Tech-
    nical Information Service, March 1977.

Executive Office of the President, Federal Coordinating Council
    for Science Engineering and Technology, Directory of
    federal technology transfer. Washington, D.C.: U.S.
    Government Printing Office, 1977.

Fairweather, G. W. Methods for experimental social innovation.
    New York: Wiley, 1967.

Fairweather, G. W. Social psychology in the treatment of men-
    tal illness: An experimental approach. New York: Wiley,
    1964.

Fairweather, G. W., Sanders, D. H., Maynard, H., and
    Cressler, D. Community life for the mentally ill. Chica-
    go: Aldine, 1969.

Fairweather, G. W., Sanders, D. H., and Tornatzky, L. G.
    Creating change in mental health organizations. New
    York: Pergamon Press, 1974.

Fairweather, G. W., and Tornatzky, L. G. Experimental
    methods for social policy research. Oxford: Pergamon
    Press, 1977.

Fawcett, R. Fairweather Friends. Southwest Airlines Maga-
    zine, 7, no. 12 (1978): 28-37.

Ferguson, C. Concerning the nature of human systems and
    the consultant's role. Journal of Applied Behavioral
    Science, 4, no. 2 (March/April 1969): 186.

Festinger, L. A theory of social comparison processes.
    Human Relations, 7 (1954): 117-146.

Freedman, J. L., and Fraser, C. C. Compliance without pressure: The foot in the door technique. Journal of Personality and Social Psychology, 4 (1966): 195-202.

French, J. R. P., Israel, J. and As, D. An experiment on participation in a Norwegian factory. Human Relations, 13, no. 1 (1960): 3-19.

French, W., and Bell, C. Organization development: Behavorial science intervention for organization improvement. Englewood Cliffs, N.J.: Prentice-Hall, 1973.

Galbraith, J. Designing complex organizations. Reading, Mass.: Addition-Wesley, 1973.

Giacquinta, J. B. Educational innovation in schools: Some distressing conclusions about implementation. Paper presented at the meeting of the American Educational Research Association, Toronto, Canada, 1978.

Glaser, E. M. and Backer, T. E. Innovation redefined: durability and local adaptation. Evaluation, 4 (1977): 131-135.

Glaser, E. M., and Ross, H. L. Increasing the utilization of applied research results. Los Angeles: Human Interaction Research Institute, 1971.

Guilford, J. P. Psychometric methods. 2nd ed. New York: McGraw-Hill, 1954.

Gross, J., Giacquinta, J. B., and Berstein, . Implementing organizational innovations. New York: Basic Books, 1971.

Hage, J., and Aiken, M. Social change in complex organizations. New York: Random House, 1970.

Hall, G., and Loucks, S. F. A developmental model for determining whether the treatment is actually implemented. American Educational Research Journal, 14, no. 3 (1977): 263-276.

Hanson, P. G. Individual and group effectiveness training: A handbook for trainers. Washington, D.C. Dept. of Medicine and Surgery, Veterans Administration, June 1973.

Harris, R. N. The diffusion of the community lodge. Unpublished dissertation, Michigan State University, 1973.

Havelock, R. G. Planning for innovation through dissemination and utilization of knowledge. Ann Arbor, Mich.: Center for Research on Utilization of Scientific Knowledge, Institute for Social Research, University of Michigan, 1971.

Havelock, R. G. Training for change agents. Center for Research on Utilization of Scientific Knowledge, Institute for Social Research, University of Michigan, Ann Arbor, 1972.

Havelock, R. G., and Havelock, M. Educational innovation in the United States: Vol. 1: The national survey: The substance and the process. Ann Arbor, Mich.: Institute for Social Research, University of Michigan, 1973.

Hovland, C. I., Janis, I. L., and Kelley, H. H. Communication and persuasion. New Haven, Conn.: Yale University Press, 1953.

Hovland, C. I., and Weiss, W. The influence of source credibility on communication effectiveness. Public Opinion Quarterly, 15 (1951): 635-650.

Huse, E. F. Organization development and change. St. Paul, Minn.: West Pub. Co., 1975.

Johns, E. A. The sociology of organizational change. Oxford: Pergamon Press, 1973.

Kaufman, H. Are government organizations immortal? Washington, D.C.: The Brookings Institute, 1976.

Kirst, M. W. The new politics of state education finance. Phi Delta Kappan (February 1979): 427-432.

Lambright, W. H. Adoption and utilization of urban technology: A decision-making study. Syracuse Research Corporation, Syracuse, N.Y., 1977.

La Piere, R. T. Social change. New York: McGraw-Hill, 1965.

Larsen, J. K., Arutunian, C. A., and Finley, C. J. Diffusion of innovations among community mental health centers. (AIR-29800 & 38100-8/74-FR). Palo Alto, Calif.: American Institutes for Research, 1974.

Lawrence, P. R., and Lorsch, J. W. Organization and environment. Boston: Harvard Business School, 1967.

Lewin, K. Group decision and social change. In E. Maccoby, T. M. Newcomb, and E. L. Hartley (eds.), Readings in social psychology. New York: Henry Holt & Co., 1958.

Litwak, E. Models of bureaucracy that permit conflict. American Journal of Sociology, 57 (September 1961): 173-183.

Lounsbury, J. W. The diffusion of environmental action practices: A community experiment. International Review of Applied Psychology, 25, no. 1 (1976): 15-21.

March, J. G., and Simon, H. A. Organizations. Pittsburgh, Pa.: Graduate School of Industrial Administration, Carnegie Institute of Technology, 1958.

McKelvey, B. Guidelines for an empirical classification of organizations. Administrative Science Quarterly, 20 (December 1975): 509-525.

McLuhan, M. Understanding Media. New York: McGraw-Hill, 1964.

Merton, R. K. Social theory and social structure. London: The Free Press of Glencoe, 1957.

Morris, W.C., and Sashkin, M. Organization behavior in action. Skill building experiences. St. Paul, Minn.: West Pub. Co., 1976.

Palmore, J. Chicago snowball: A study of the flow and diffusion of family planning information. In D. Bogue (ed.), Sociological contributions to family planning research. Chicago: University of Chicago Community and Family Study Center, 1967.

Perrow, C. Complex organizations: A critical essay. Glenview, Ill.: Scott, Foresman, & Co., 1972.

Pfeiffer, J. W., and Jones, J. L. A handbook of structured experiences for human relations training, vols. I-IV. La Jolla, Calif.: University Associates and Consultants, 1969, 1970a, 1970b, and 1973.

Pincus, J. Incentives of innovation in the public schools. Review of Educational Research, 44 no. 1, (1974): 113-114.

President's Commission on Mental Health, Report to the president from the president's commission on mental health, vol. II, Washington, D.C.: U.S. Government Printing Office, 1978.

Richards, W. D. A manual for network analysis. Unpublished manuscript. Stanford University, Stanford, Calif. Institute for Communication Research, 1975.

Richland, M. Final report: Traveling seminar and conference for the implementation of educational innovations. (ERIC No. 003126). Systems Development Corporation, 1965.

Roethlisberger, F. J., and Dickson, W. J. Management and the worker. Cambridge, Mass.: Harvard University Press, 1947.

Rogers, E. M. Innovation in organizations: New research approaches. Paper presented at the meeting of the American Political Science Association, San Francisco, Calif., September 1975.

Rogers, E. M., and Agarwala-Rogers, R. Communication in organizations. New York: Free Press, 1976.

Rogers, E. M., and Shoemaker, F. F. Communication of innovation: A cross-cultural approach. 2nd ed. New York: The Free Press, 1971.

Ryan, B. and Gross, N. C. The diffusion of hybrid seed corn in two Iowa communities. Rural Sociology, 8 (1943): 15-24.

Salasin, S. Experimentation revisited: A conversation with Donald T. Campbell. Evaluation, 1, no. 3 (1973): 9-10.

Schacter, S. The psychology of affiliation. Stanford: Stanford University Press, 1959.

Schein, E. Process consultation: Its role in organization development. Reading, Mass.: Addison-Wesley, 1969.

Scheirer, M. A. Program participants' positive perceptions. Evaluation Quarterly, 2, no. 1 (February 1978): 53-70.

Schon, D. Beyond the stable state: public and private learning in a changing society. London: Temple Smith, 1971.

Stevens, W. and Tornatzky, L. The dissemination of evaluation: An experiment. Evaluation Quarterly, 1980, in press.

Tannenbaum, A. S. (ed.) Control in Organizations. New York: McGraw-Hill, 1968.

Taylor, J., and Bowers, D. Survey of organizations: A machine-scored standardized quetionnaire instrument. Ann Arbor, Mich.: Institute for Social Research, University of Michigan, 1972.

Thompson, J. D. Organizations in action. New York: McGraw-Hill, 1967.

Tornatzky, L. G., Avellar, J. W., Fergus, E. O., Fleischer, M., and Fairweather, G. W. The small group ward program. East Lansing, Mich.: Michigan State University, 1978.

Tryon, R. C., and Bailey, D. C. Cluster analysis. New York: McGraw-Hill, 1970.

Turner, J. C., and TenHoor, W. J. The NIMH community support program: Pilot approach to a needed social reform. Schizophrenia Bulletin, 4, no. 3 (1978): 319-344.

Weber, M. Theory of social and economic organization. (A. M. Henderson and T. Parsons, eds. and trans.). New York: Oxford University Press, 1947.

Weiss, C. Using social research in public policy making. Lexington, Mass.: D. C. Heath, 1977.

Williams, W. Social policy research and analysis. New York: Elsevier, 1971.

Winer, B. J. Statistical principles in experimental design. 2nd ed. New York: McGraw-Hill, 1971.

Yin, R. K. Changing urban bureaucracies: How new practices become routinized. Executive Summary. Washington, D.C.: Rand Corporation, 1978.

Zaltman, G., & Duncan, R. Strategies for planned change. New York: John Wiley & Sons, 1977.

Index

217

About the Authors

LOUIS G. TORNATZKY is Group Leader, Innovation Processes and their Management, Division of Policy Research and Analysis, National Science Foundation. Prior to joining the NSF he was Professor of Urban and Metropolitan Studies and Psychology, Michigan State University. He has written extensively on field experimentation in policy research and program evaluation. Dr. Tornatzky received his Ph.D. in Psychology from Stanford University.

ESTHER O. FERGUS is Assistant Professor of Education and Psychology, Michigan State University. She received her Ph.D. in Ecological Psychology from Michigan State University, and her B.Ed. from the University of Hawaii. Her interests are in innovation processes and in problems of the elderly.

JOSEPH W. AVELLAR is Director, Office of Program Standards, and Evaluation, Virginia Department of Mental Health and Mental Retardation. He received his Ph.D. in Social-Community Psychology at the University of California, Riverside. He is interested in community-based programs for the mentally ill and in program evaluation.

GEORGE W. FAIRWEATHER is Professor, Department of Psychology, Michigan State University, where he directs the graduate program in Ecological Psychology. He has a long involvement in field experimental research addressed to significant social issues. Dr. Fairweather received his Ph.D. in Psychology and Sociology from the University of Illinois.

MITCHELL FLEISCHER is Assistant Professor, Department of Psychology, Indiana University of Pennsylvania, and Director of the Community Psychology Graduate Program there. He received his Ph.D. in Ecological Psychology from Michigan State University.